Confessions of an Ex-Pentecostal

Confessions of an Ex-Pentecostal by Phil Stairs carefully recounts his long and agonizing quest to find his home in the evangelical world. Raised in the United Pentecostal Church by his godly father with very strong friendships therein, Phil, being a reflective thinker, began to have doubts and ambivalent feelings about the UPC. This book is well-written, self-effacing, humorous at times and irenic, in the spirit of Proverbs 27:6: "Faithful are the wounds of a friend." Throughout the book Phil remains a friend of Pentecostals while exposing their weaknesses and praising their strengths, seeking always to base his perspective on Scripture. May God be pleased to use it to promote unity in the family of God.

Rick Cryder
Chaplain and retired pastor, Hamilton, Ohio, USA

Confessions of an Ex-Pentecostal is a fascinating story of the personal and theological struggles of a pastor brought up in one of the more extreme representations of Pentecostalism. It is a story filled with love toward those from whom he eventually separated. This book is devoid of anger and bitterness but filled with thoughtfulness and a desire to follow God wherever that would lead. While the title would not seem to endear itself to Pentecostals, the struggles and his charitable heart will likely be an encouragement to such. Phil takes us on a journey of the soul that is intriguing and thought provoking. I expect godly people of a number of different persuasions will find this short book long on blessing and encouragement.

Doug Blair
Retired pastor, former chair of Heritage College & Seminary and former chair of the Fellowship National Council

I enjoyed reading my friend and brother Phil Stairs' story of his personal, theological and pastoral journey. Phil writes as he was in person: brief, blunt, astute, with a wonderfully dry sense of humour. In our age of unquestioned and unabashed partisanship, it was truly refreshing to see how Phil tried to get each side of the aisle to learn from the other—something sorely lacking in most debates today. I commend *Confessions of an Ex-Pentecostal* to charismatics and non-charismatics alike.

Wayne Baxter
Professor of New Testament and Greek, Heritage College & Seminary

Mentored into pastoral ministry by Phil Stairs and remaining close friends for nearly another thirty years, I noted that there were two things that were the construct of his life—he never took himself seriously and always took his Lord and Saviour, Jesus, very seriously. In so many ways *Confessions of an Ex-Pentecostal* is the fruit of that reality. Phil was a man who lived to demythologize pretense and ministered from a platform of earthy spirituality. Thirty-five years ago, Phil entrusted me with the deeper realities of his life when he handed me the manuscript to this book. He never published it for reasons that remain his own. I am glad his family is choosing to publish this page-turner—it is a journey worth sharing. It is no small thing to offramp a generational belief system.

Rick Baker
Retired pastor, Fellowship National Council Member and ABWE Board Member

Though Phil is no longer physically with us, he still has much to teach us all through this book's humble wisdom and vulnerable transparency concerning his own personal experience and eventual departure from his traditional Pentecostal upbringing.

Tim Roddick
Pastor, Trailhead Baptist Church, Petawawa, Ontario, Canada

Phil's struggle in his life and ministry was caused by his commitment to "a real exegetical base" for his beliefs and his unwavering duty to doctrinal integrity. How we pray that every pastor would be driven by these same convictions, for then they would experience what Phil did: a life spent well for God's gospel glory.

This story will bless Christians, and certainly pastors, as in it you will learn from one whose sole authority was the Word of God for all of life and ministry. Calling you to be men and women of the Book, guided, directed and constrained by the Word. This was true for Phil to such a degree that it demanded significant change in his life and ministry—at great personal and relational cost. However, this was a cost he was willing to pay, to be faithful to the Word of Christ and the Christ of the Word.

Norm Millar
Senior pastor, Redemption Bible Chapel, London, Ontario, Canada

I first met Phil as a new youth pastor near the beginning of my pastoral vocation. I ventured out to our Fellowship Baptist Association meeting in London, Ontario, and knew no one. Seasoned senior pastors were enjoying one another's company, with very few leaders in attendance who looked like me. After a few visits, I thought of not returning—except for Pastor Stairs. He searched me out at each gathering and spent time talking and praying with me. We had lost our lead pastor, and I needed help and wisdom; I needed a sounding board. Phil wonderfully provided that for me, with much grace and encouragement. I deeply appreciated him.

I knew nothing of Pastor Stair's background until many years later. What I experienced in my early days of ministry was his immense shepherding heart and his generous spirit. In his book, *Confessions of an Ex-Pentecostal*, amid the struggles he faced and the burden of deciding to exit his faith family, I was wonderfully reminded of his generous and gracious spirit toward all people, even those he strongly disagreed with on matters of doctrine. A true gentle-man.

Steven Jones
National president, The Fellowship of Evangelical Baptist Churches in Canada

One of my favourite memories of Phil Stairs is when I tried to imitate Eugene Peterson's "Kittel Among the Coffee Cups."[1] For a number of months, on Tuesday mornings, a group of six to eight of us would gather to translate from the Greek New Testament (the Gospel of Mark) and exchange ideas and reflections. Phil was a leader in this group who always came with a precise translation, a researched interpretation and thoughtful reflections on implication and impact. This was very much rooted in his high view of Scripture, his passion for biblical preaching and his commitment to the ministry and mission of Christ's church. These values are very much reflected in his very personal story recounted in this book. The values that Phil embraced are a reminder of how important such values are when any of us seek to do well in our callings as pastors and teachers.

David G. Barker
Professor emeritus of biblical studies, Heritage College & Seminary, Cambridge, Ontario, Canada

---

[1] A chapter in Eugene H. Peterson, *Subversive Spirituality* (Grand Rapids: Eerdmans, 1997).

Philip D. Stairs (1941–2019)

CONFESSIONS
OF AN EX-PENTECOSTAL

Philip D. Stairs

HERITAGE SEMINARY PRESS

Heritage Seminary Press, Cambridge, Ontario
An imprint of H&E Publishing, West Lorne, Ontario, Canada

heritageseminarypress.com

© 2025 Lelia Stairs. All rights reserved. This book may not be reproduced, in whole or in part, without written permission from the publishers.

Edited by Lelia Stairs, Stephanie (Stairs) Roddick and Jonathan Stairs
Cover & book design by Janice Van Eck

Unless otherwise indicated, Scripture quotations are from the ESV® Bible (The Holy Bible, English Standard Version®), © 2001 by Crossway, a publishing ministry of Good News Publishers. Used by permission. All rights reserved.

Confessions of an Ex-Pentecostal
By Philip D. Stairs

ISBN 978-1-77484-180-8 (paperback)
ISBN 978-1-77484-181-5 (eBook)

This book is dedicated to all those who do not feel they fit in, who are trying to align their beliefs with God's Word and are willing to lovingly sacrifice relationships to follow hard after Christ. As Phil would say, "I would rather be right than liked."

Contents

Foreword by David A. Reed	xiii
Preface	xvii
1 Uprooted	1
2 Shaken foundations	15
3 An identity crisis	31
4 One of them	45
5 Why I left	61
6 Is this that?	71
7 What are the best gifts?	83
8 A second work?	91
9 Problems in the upper room	103
10 Can we learn from each other?	115
Epilogue by Jonathan Stairs	125
Acknowledgements	129
Appendix A: Words of praise to receive the Holy Ghost	131
Appendix B: Letter from the UPC superintendent E.P. Wickens	133
Appendix C: "Why I am still Pentecostal?"	135
Bibliography	137

Foreword

P hil and I knew well an old Pentecostal favourite, "This world is not my home, I'm just a-passing through." I'm sure we sang it hundreds of times in our little village churches in New Brunswick, Canada. We would sing it on Sunday mornings and at Sunday evening evangelistic services. We sang it at area fellowship meetings and summer camps. We both knew we did not belong here. In the fifties, we knew for certain we did not belong with those other "dry-as-last-year's-bird's-nest" churches. They were just way too much at home here!

The truth is, we were not a-passing through alone. We were not solo travellers. We cherished fellowship with the "brethren," which of course included the sisters! We were in church Sunday mornings, Sunday evenings, midweek Bible study, prayer meetings and more. Many of us "holy rollers" felt like Abraham and Sarah, embarking on a trip with the destination still a blank. It was like passing through towns of strangers. We pitched our tents (literally, the "revival tent meetings"), and some joined us.

Phil and I also shared this: we were "Oneness" Pentecostals.[1] Our tribe could sometimes be exclusive and was often excluded. We dared to denounce the "three gods" of the Trinitarians, and were ready to face their persecuting wrath. We accused them of believing that the three persons in the Godhead must *de facto* mean three separate centres of consciousness—anathema to both sides of course. Claiming to be biblically consistent, we baptized as the apostles instructed us: invoking God's revealed name, Jesus. The generic titles, Father, Son and Holy Spirit were not proper names. These "apostolic truths" made us distinctive, and sometimes peculiar. Yet it was baffling, since each side recognized—sometimes only silently—a common love for Jesus and an experience of the same Holy Spirit in the face of the other. Some showed it; others harboured it. Phil and I showed it.

That is who we were when we met. Phil's family moved to Fredericton in 1957. We ended up in the same class, the only "holy rollers," and both came from clergy families. There was something special about the bond that held us together for the next sixty-two years. Our paths converged and sometimes

---

[1] Oneness or "Jesus Name" Pentecostalism (sometimes incorrectly labelled "Jesus Only") was an accident of history, sort of. It was the last wave of a Christocentric shift in the revival's first decade. Events began with a little book by a premillennial fundamentalist who taught that the modern dead church would regain its spiritual power if it would only return to the apostolic practice of baptizing in the name of the Lord Jesus Christ. Here the compound name was the name of the Trinity in revelation. This little book soon passed into the hands of a Pentecostal evangelist and eventually made its way into a camp meeting baptismal sermon. Another Pentecostal evangelist heard the sermon, ruminated on it for a year, then launched a tent meeting revival with a radically new message. This message was different. The singularity of Jesus in name and identity reduced the doctrine of the Trinity to temporal manifestations only. The reason? Divine "persons" carried all the modern baggage of singular identities, and had to be rejected for its tritheistic insinuations. Now God's eternal nature would be singular, and the only salvific and therefore acceptable name in baptism was Jesus.

Oneness Pentecostals are not all cut from the same cloth. Some believe that one is saved through the sinner's prayer. Others believe the new birth requires repentance, water baptism in the name of Jesus Christ and the Pentecostal experience of Spirit baptism with speaking in tongues. The latter often offer "two buses" to heaven: those with the full Pentecostal experience can get on the first bus; those who only repent have to wait for the second bus and likely endure a period of persecution. Some worship with Trinitarians, others only cooperate on projects. The global strength of Oneness Pentecostals is estimated at 20–25 million. A global tour will reveal some surprises: babies being baptized, babies being immersed in a river, feet being washed as a sacrament, worshipping on the Sabbath, handling serpents and more.

diverged. We both stepped outside our Pentecostal family, Phil to the Baptists, me to the Anglicans. We both excelled academically to earn our doctorates, and both served in pastoral ministry for many years. But we never lost sight of each other. We accepted each other, occasionally irritated each other, but loved each other to the end. And I still miss him dearly, my lifelong friend.

Phil's memoir is much more than a personal story. He knew—instinctively and spiritually—"Until you are at home somewhere, you cannot be at home anywhere."[2] He traces for us his sometimes painful search, to find a more fitting spiritual home on this side of heaven. It took time, patience, discouragement and discernment. Having found it, his life and ministry bore fruit in abundance.

We never lose the language of our spiritual birth. Even as Phil served in another Christian community for most of his life, one could occasionally detect a subtle but familiar cadence from an earlier time. Phil knew that his former Pentecostal home could still be a bearer of blessing for many. For himself, he had decided to be an "Ex-", but something lingered...sometimes he even sounded like his daddy in the middle of a sermon!

Wisdom awaits the reader.

David A. Reed
Professor emeritus of pastoral theology and research professor
Wycliffe College, University of Toronto

---

[2] Mary C. Bateson

Preface

The late Dr. Addison Leitch was a favourite professor of mine while pursuing studies at Gordon-Conwell Theological Seminary. I remember him complaining about evangelicals who were "kicking their mother." By that remark, he referred to students converted and nurtured in fundamental Bible churches who were now very critical of their fundamentalist roots.

I do not want to kick my mother, the church that gave me birth. Rather, I hope it will be seen as a gentle shake from an appreciative friend. The main reason for my delay in writing about my feelings was not wanting to give my physical parents more embarrassment. It was difficult for them to accept my breaking ranks with the Pentecostal[1] brethren. Putting it all into

---

[1] References to "Pentecostal" are to the United Pentecostal Church (UPC). UPC beliefs can be found at https://upci.org/our-beliefs/. The UPC Church in Canada has its roots when, "In 1917, Aimee Semple McPherson from Salford, Ontario came to

print would have added to their misery. They are both in heaven now and I think they understand.

The position presented in this book is not one that will likely receive unanimous endorsement from either side of the charismatic divide. I sort of feel like the soldier I heard about from the Civil War period. It seems he could not make up his mind which side to be on so he put on a blue tunic from the North and grey pants from the South. The result was he got shot at from both sides. I have definitely taken sides, but I still have enough of my Pentecostal clothing left on to get shot at from both sides.

That precisely is the contribution I hope to make. I have been there and left. My present position is almost a 180-degree turn. At the same time, I have retained my admiration and affection for Pentecostals. There is no bitterness in my heart toward them.

It might be a temptation to drag out some dirty linen regarding Charismatics and Pentecostals; the secular media have done a great job at that. Two reasons prevent me from joining them. First, it is the dirty linen of my brothers in Christ so in that sense it is also my dirty linen. Second, every denomination has its own laundry basket well filled. To point a finger would invite having one point back. Therefore, it would be counterproductive and only lead to more misunderstanding.

I have no illusions that the gulf between Pentecostals and other denominations can be bridged. The differences are too great to hope that they might be brought under one roof. Our separate fellowships are necessary, like fences between farms. However, the farmers need not fight and might even learn from one another.

---

the area of Bangor, Maine, and parts of New Brunswick and some Baptist pastors attended her meetings receiving their personal Pentecost." See Ralph Reynolds & Joyce Morehouse, *From the Rising of the Sun. A History of the Apostolic Truth Across Canada and the Reflections of a Pioneer Preacher* (Surrey: Conexions, 1998), 29. Interestingly, "it was another Baptist holiness minister William Seymour, a descendant of African slaves who travelled from Texas to Los Angeles and set up shop at 312 Azusa Street and started preaching. On April 9, 1906, they had an experience whereby they claimed they received the 'Baptism of the Holy Spirit,' which began the modern day Pentecostal movement." See "The Azusa Street Revival," in Robert J. Morgan, *On This Day: 365 Amazing and Inspiring Stories about Saints, Martyrs and Heroes* (Nashville: Thomas Nelson, 1997).

A two-fold purpose has prompted me to expose myself in a way that goes against my nature. One is a desire to cause Pentecostals to examine what I see as obvious flaws in the system. The other purpose is to urge reflection on the part of those moving in a Pentecostal direction as a solution to all of their problems. If I cannot supply answers, I am prepared to settle with creating questions.

Philip D. Stairs
1989[2]

---

[2] This book was completed by 1989, but first published in 2025 (this edition).

1

Uprooted

A threatening sky greeted me as I stepped outside of the church on that last Monday in December 1970. I had just completed my last task as pastor. The previous evening, I had preached my farewell message from Philippians 2:12. The next morning I returned to the church to give a final coat of varnish to the doors leading from the foyer to the main auditorium. Less than three months before, we had moved into the new church. We had decided to finish it by volunteer labour, and I ended up being the main volunteer. Those doors needed a final coat because of heavy usage, and I was afraid nobody would do it after I left.

When I completed my task, I cleaned the brush and put the brush and can of varnish away. Then I walked through the church for the last time, looking at that building which had been my dream since arriving as pastor and which had been a reality for such a brief time. I locked the door behind me and stood for a

2 Confessions of an Ex-Pentecostal

St. Stephen Pentecostal Church, St. Stephen, New Brunswick, 1970.

moment while removing the key from the ring so I could pass it on. As I stood there, I made the decision to leave town later that afternoon to avoid getting storm-stayed. December 1970 had been one of the worst months for snow in Eastern Canada in memory. Standing on the steps of the church I thought briefly about what had transpired over the past few weeks. It almost seemed unreal, and I could hardly believe I had carried through my decision to leave. It was like a dream, and not a pleasant one. In essence, I had been going through the motions of doing what had to be done: resigning as pastor, obtaining a visa to enter the United States, moving our furniture and helping the church find a new pastor. It was much like the feeling I would have a decade later in making and carrying out funeral arrangements for my parents who passed away a little more than two years apart. You do what has to be done.

Leaving a pastorate—for whatever reason—is never easy. There is a finality about it. No matter how we talk about still "being friends for life," the fact is, most of the congregation passes out of your life and you out of theirs. This particular transition was no ordinary move though. It was a case of:

Uprooted 3

St. Stephen parsonage

> Two roads diverged in a woods and I—
> I took the one less traveled by,
> And that has made all the difference.[1]

To begin with, I was leaving my hometown: a border town between New Brunswick and Maine where I had been born. For sixteen years it had been my home. Ten years later, I returned to the parsonage of my childhood, only now as pastor. My parents lived in the same town and had been so delighted to have my wife Lelia and me close. The rest of the family was scattered throughout North America, from Florida to northwestern Ontario. A week later my father would turn seventy, and we were needed. But for now, the moment I dreaded was only hours away. Toward evening I would announce it was time to go. We had been staying with my parents since moving our furniture to the United States a couple of weeks prior, between snowstorms. My dad would

---

[1] The last lines of Robert Frost's poem, "The Road Not Taken."

The old St. Stephen Church.

insist we pray before departure, so the four of us would kneel down in the living room. Dad and Lelia would cry. Mother and I would keep a brave front and choke back the tears, but inside we would be broken up. Then we would hug, hurry to the car and quickly drive out of town, across the border going as far as Bangor, Maine, that first night. The gloom of the darkness as we left that night, seemed fitting with the gloom I felt inside.

We were also leaving my home church. I had been brought up in the church my father had founded in 1927. He pastored there until becoming director of the Foreign Missions Department within his denomination in 1945. The rest of the family remained in St. Stephen, New Brunswick, while my father worked out of the denominational headquarters in St. Louis, Missouri. We would have a part-time father for the remainder of our growing-up years.

My father's replacement was not able to fit in and left within the first year. My mother supplied the pulpit and the church eventually called her as their pastor. She would remain as pastor for eleven years until her health no longer allowed in 1957. I would be

The church I pastored on Grand Manan Island.

converted at the age of five under my mother's ministry, and she would become the dominant parental and pastoral influence in my formative years. I am the only man I know who has the dubious distinction of being told that he "preaches like his mother."[2]

In 1957, our family would leave St. Stephen and move to Fredericton. My dad would later return to St. Stephen as pastor in 1964 after the church had declined considerably. In 1967, Dad would retire and recommend me as his replacement. At that time, I was pastoring a small church on Grand Manan Island in the Bay of Fundy. I would accept the call to my home church with considerable trepidation.

For one thing, I received only an 80 per cent vote, meaning 20 per cent of the voting members did not want me as their pastor. I cannot say that I blamed them. I was one of the kids they knew as a baby. Some of the ladies had even changed my diapers, and it would be difficult for them to think of me as their pastor. It could well be a case of a prophet having honour everywhere but in his own country and house (Mark 6:4).

---

[2] Phil believed in the protective and sacrificial leadership of men in the home and church. He was a committed complementarian after he left the Pentecostals and believed the role of elder and pastor was reserved for men only. He would have said that the role of pastor fell to his mother and this took its toll on her, the marriage and the health of the family.

My father had also changed his views and moderated some extreme positions of his earlier ministry. This had created some confusion in the church, particularly among some of the older members. They would say, "If it was true back then, why isn't it true now?" However, in spite of these difficulties, and knowing that I would not have the honeymoon period usually afforded to new pastors, I accepted the call of the church, ultimately believing it to be the call of God.

To the surprise of many, including myself, the next three-and-a-half years would be some of the happiest and most fruitful years of my ministry. There was none of the usual "wearing a mask" or "putting on a good face" for the new pastor. These people knew me and I knew them so there were no pretences. We simply got right down to business. The church became harmonious and experienced rapid growth. The new church building, to replace the hall-like structure, which I dreamed about from the beginning, became an obvious necessity. Land was purchased and a building fund commenced. A few months before starting construction I had decided to take a secret ballot vote of confidence to see if the people wanted me to continue as pastor. I felt this was an important consideration before actually commencing the building program. In a miracle at the very least rivalling the changing of water to wine, I received a 100 per cent vote of confidence. Some who had initially voted against my pastoral call told me they now voted for me to remain because they had seen God's blessing on our church since my arrival.

Many people thought I would be there for life. After all, a father, a mother and now a son almost constituted a dynasty. A packed auditorium, on the day we opened our new church building in October 1970, seemed only to confirm that I would be there for a long time, if not for life. The excitement of that opening day was not shared by me however, and only my wife and parents knew that I was weighed down with a decision to leave this beloved church that was so much a part of me.

More significant than leaving my hometown and my parents, or even leaving my home church, was that I was leaving my life-long denomination. I was brought up Pentecostal. My father was one of the pioneers of the Pentecostal movement in Eastern Canada. He became a top executive in the international

My parents, Margaret and Wynn Stairs, and me.

organization that was formed in 1945. Although he lost his position in 1962 due to political judgement on his part, he was an enthusiastic Pentecostal minister until his death in 1982. I had followed my father's footsteps and was ordained as a minister of the United Pentecostal Church (UPC) in 1969.

Historically, the UPC is one of the most radical Pentecostal organizations. They hold a controversial belief that denies the Trinity and they are known as a "Jesus Only" denomination.[3] Most teach that both water baptism in Jesus' name and Spirit baptism with the evidence of speaking in other tongues are what constitute the new birth described by Jesus in John 3:3 and 3:5, "Truly, truly, I say to you, unless one is born again he cannot see the kingdom of God." The UPC also holds to a very legalistic

---

[3] The UPC would be classified as "Oneness Pentecostals." Oneness Pentecostals most famous pastor was T.D. Jakes until he transitioned to believe in the Trinity (see https://www.christianitytoday.com/news/2012/january/td-jakes-embraces-doctrine-of-trinity-moves-away-from.html).

code of conduct, forbidding women to cut their hair, wear make-up or wear slacks.

The move I would make would be a relatively small step geographically, only about 600 kilometres (or 350 miles), but theologically, it would be a giant step. The last Sunday of December 1970 I would be the pastor of a church affiliated with the UPC. One week later I would be pastoring a suburban Boston church affiliated with the American Baptist Convention, known by some as the most liberal Baptist denomination in the United States.

The move would be so radical that years later, a pulpit committee that received a verbal profile of me from a friend, thought there was some mistake. The chairman of the deacons said: "This fellow is supposed to have been an ordained UPC minister, pastored an American Baptist Church, graduated from Moody Bible Institute and Westminster Theological Seminary; all that doesn't go together. It can't be the same fellow!" I expect a millennium or two hence, any historian reading my obituary would consider it to be a multiplicity of sources put together into one document!

Leaving my Pentecostal affiliation was not easy. It was leaving my roots—and they were roots that I loved. There is a comradery among Pentecostals in general and Pentecostal ministers in particular, that was very close. They were not only my associates, but my friends. We had worked together, prayed together, raised money for mission projects together, laughed together and wept together. Although I was considered suspect when I returned to my home district after attending "anti-Pentecostal" schools, the brethren had accepted me. I was kindly and fairly treated, even by those who would consider me soft on Pentecostal doctrine. The opportunity to teach in the official UPC Bible Institute was given to me on a part-time basis for three years. In the summer of 1970, I was asked to preach in a morning service at the district Camp Meeting, something considered an honour.

Leaving all of this behind, I was heading into unknown territory. Never again would I have the same sense of belonging. It was especially painful to know that "my brethren" would use me as an illustration for sermons on everyone from Esau to Demas, and maybe even Judas. I had known all the leaders of our denomination from childhood, most of whom had spent time in our home.

West Medford Baptist Church in Medford, Massachusetts

While at the time I might not have admitted it, I desperately wanted their approval.

It was unlikely I would ever leave the Pentecostals because of my attachment, but even more so because of my experience. I had made a commitment to Christ at the age of five. After that, I was told I should seek for the "baptism of the Holy Ghost,"[4] which would be accompanied by the evidence of speaking in other tongues as described in Acts 2:4. While my sins were

---

[4] "The baptism of the Holy Ghost (Spirit)" or "the baptism" for short as the UPC described it, is considered by the UPC as the evidence of salvation, namely, the speaking of tongues. Phil came to believe the baptism of the Holy Spirit described in John 1:33, Acts 1:5, *et al* occurs at the moment of salvation and speaking in tongues is not the ultimate nor the necessary evidence of the baptism of the Holy Spirit.

forgiven, I needed the baptism to make me part of the Bride, the Church, and ready for the rapture. Lacking it, I might miss the rapture, have to go through the Great Tribulation, refuse the mark of the Beast, be beheaded and then I might go to heaven (Revelation 13). It was not a chance I wanted to take so I started seeking the baptism of the Holy Ghost. In addition, I was told the baptism would give me power to overcome sin in my daily life.

For four years the experience eluded me. Every Sunday night I would respond to the altar call and go down to the prayer room to seek the baptism. I watched others receive the experience and speak in tongues, but for some reason I was unable to "let go." Older saints (as we called them) gathered around me, laid hands on me, prayed for me and encouraged me to "let go," but to no avail.

Finally, in March 1951, at nine years of age, I received it. We had a men's prayer meeting on Saturday nights and I faithfully attended it. In the absence of my father, some of the men would pick me up and take me home. We did nothing but pray for at least a couple of hours. This particular night I was praying for my baptism of the Spirit as usual, but this time it would be different. I began to pray more fervently. After a while, I fell over on my back and was "slain in the Spirit," as we called it. I am not sure if this action was learned or impromptu. I had seen it happen to others who received the baptism of the Spirit, so maybe I allowed it to happen as the thing to do. For certain, what later followed was not learned behaviour.

The men gathered around me and prayed for the Lord to fill me. As I lay there praying, even though I felt completely in control of my faculties, I gradually found my English becoming blurred and soon I was speaking in another language. It is hard to describe the feeling. It was certainly not one of ecstasy. It was more of peace and relief that finally I had received what I had so longed for. I remember one man saying, "He sure has received the baptism. Go call Sister Stairs!"—my mother, who was the pastor at that time. When she arrived, I had finished speaking in tongues and was sitting up. Seeing her, I rushed into her arms. My mother-pastor was very happy; I was too. Mother told me she had sensed God's hand on my life, even as a baby. She always felt that God had something special planned for me.

As soon as I got home, I wrote to my father, who was on a missionary tour in Africa, to share the good news. A week or two later, in an after-service on Sunday night, the same thing happened again. I started speaking in tongues. This time we had an elderly woman who had been a missionary in Liberia for many years visiting with us. Her name was Pearl Holmes, but we all called her "Mother Holmes." She was home on furlough and was present, listening to me speak in tongues. All of a sudden, she began to weep and praise God. After I was finished, she told us that one of the tribes in Liberia, among whom she worked, had a very difficult dialect. She had never been able to master it. That night she told us that I was using or speaking it as fluently as a native and was preaching a sermon from 1 John on "God is Love." Her immediate thought was that I would be called as a missionary to that tribe in Liberia and would be able to speak the language. However, I never had an experience like it again. God has not called me to Liberia and I cannot speak a word of that language today. What it did do was entrench Pentecostalism into me so deeply, that all the arguments against speaking in tongues fell off me like water off a duck's back.

Summing it up, I was not a likely candidate to end up where I currently am: pastoring a fundamentalist Baptist church, affiliated with a very conservative Baptist fellowship known for its strong anti-charismatic stand. After several years in more liberal Baptist denominations, I moved to my present associations, and strange as it seems, for the first time since entering the ministry, I feel comfortable and in the mainstream of my denomination.

Needless to say, the move from the UPC (which some of us referred to uncharitably as the "John Birch Society"[5] of Pentecostals) to a church in the American Baptist Convention (which some of us also uncharitably called the "Apostate Baptist Convention") was not a spur of the moment decision. I struggled with it for ten years and tried to avoid it. I even wrote an article for our denomination's paper entitled "Why I Am Still Pentecostal" defending the Pentecostal position (see Appendix C).

Leaving was not a matter of bettering myself, or finding a more successful ministry. I actually left a large, thriving church

---

[5] The John Birch Society is a right-wing political group in the United States. More information about the John Birch Society can be found at https://jbs.org.

for a much smaller, dying church. I was leaving behind a denomination in which I had acceptance and even respect, in spite of being held "suspect." My ordination council was the denomination board of presbyters. My application, to which I attached a rider, created a great deal of controversy on the board because I took positions at odds with the party line. One of the board members told me, "Phil, you have education and you can be one of our leaders in a few years." The unsaid implication was, "Play ball and don't rock the boat."

What hurt most was I did not really want to be a rebel. By nature, I am not a fighter. Basically I prefer to mind my own business and let others mind theirs. More and more I was feeling like a "safecracker at a banker's convention." I struggled with what I saw as my only two options: either stay in Pentecostalism and be constantly at odds with my brethren, or quietly leave both church and denomination.

The decision to make the break was thrust upon me suddenly and unexpectedly. One evening, in the summer of 1970, while in the midst of the building construction, our phone rang shortly after Lelia and I had retired for the night. I picked up the receiver on the bedside table phone and heard a man say, "I am the chairman of the pulpit committee of the West Medford Baptist Church in Medford, Massachusetts, and we are wondering if you would consider a call to our church." A Presbyterian minister friend had given my name to a seminary classmate who was a Baptist pastor in the area. He had told his Baptist friend that I would make a good Baptist. He in turn, passed on my name to the committee. The pulpit committee arranged for me to preach in this Baptist friend's church and meet with them afterward. I agreed, as I thought it might be interesting, and I needed a few days off from the building program.

The first meeting went well and I agreed to be a candidate for the pastoral position at the church that September. I told them they would have to wait for me to get the new church building finished and I also set three conditions to accepting the call: 1) There would be no strings on my ministry; 2) I would not have to join the American Baptist Convention; and 3) I could further my education while pastoring. The call was unanimous. That was the easy part of it. The hard part was severing relations on the other end.

My friend, George Cheatle, who thought I would make a good Baptist.

When Edward VIII abdicated the throne of Great Britain in 1936, he told of the struggle he faced, knowing he would disappoint so many people. It is difficult to make a decision when people you care about will be disappointed. In the months before I made the move, I almost backed out a number of times. When I finally did announce my plans to my parents and then to the church, I also wrote a circular letter to my fellow pastors trying to explain what I was doing. I told them I wanted to further my education and I might someday be back. This was wishful thinking. In my heart I knew, when I took that "road less traveled by," it was a one-way trip. I would not be back.

My move was probably not as much of a surprise as I thought it would be. I was called "The Baptist" by a number of my Pentecostal colleagues and they did not mean it as a compliment. Before I left town in December 1970, I had already left my Pentecostal roots intellectually and emotionally. I had felt like a misfit for some time. How and why I left Pentecostalism is what I would like to share in the following pages.

2

Shaken foundations

I recognized the buildings as soon as we rounded the corner from Chicago Avenue onto LaSalle Street. I had seen their picture in the school catalog. What surprised me, was to discover that Moody Bible Institute (MBI) is located in a very busy part of the city. For some reason, I had pictured the Institute as being in a quiet section of Chicago.

It was the third week of August 1961, when I first walked through the arch into Crowell Hall and asked for directions to the admissions office. As my dad, a pastor friend and I made our way up the elevator, I was embarrassed to be applying for admission less than three weeks before the school opened. I had almost applied several times before so I knew, due to limited space, only one in three applications was accepted.

My interest in MBI had developed about three years earlier. A book published by the Moody Press had made a great impact on my life. Following my Pentecostal experience at the age of nine, I struggled with a problem that I could not talk about because I was under the impression it should not exist. I still sinned! Mind you, confessing my sinful life would hardly form the basis for a new daytime soap opera, but it bothered me. I still struggled with anger, resentment, unkind feelings, not always being completely honest and, when I entered my teen years, with impure thoughts. I was embarrassed for being the only one in my class at school who could not go to the movies and had to go to church several times a week. I was especially embarrassed at being called a "holy roller." My mother told me I should not play Little League baseball as it was with a "worldly crowd," but still I wanted to play. I would slip out sometimes and play for the Holy Rosary team from the Catholic school (after all "holy rosary" and "holy roller" sounded quite similar). I felt guilty about it but I loved it. All of this seemed incompatible with being "filled with Spirit."

The testimony service at our church left the impression that Spirit-filled Christians never sinned, always witnessed and lived constantly on the high of a spiritual mountain top. I did not! One of our favourite songs was entitled "The Hallelujah Side."[1] One stanza declares:

> Here the sun is always shining
> Here the sky is always bright;
> 'Tis no place for gloomy Christians to abide,
> For my soul is filled with music
> And my heart with great delight
> And I'm living on the hallelujah side.

It seemed to me I was frequently offside. We would sing the chorus, "Every day with Jesus is sweeter than the day before, Every day with Jesus, I love him more and more"[2] but some days went sour and I seemed to love him less. I was experiencing the struggles of Romans 7 and did not understand it. I was sure I must be a hypocrite. The only way out was to "backslide," a rather frequent occurrence around our church. I considered backsliding for a few years until I was, say twenty-one—beyond the age of

---

[1] Johnson Oatman, "The Hallelujah Side," 1898.
[2] Robert Claire Loveless, "Every Day with Jesus is Sweeter than the Day Before," 1936.

having fun—then maybe I could make it as a Christian. But I did not want to backslide, I wanted to serve the Lord.

This struggle continued until at the age of seventeen when I picked up a book in my father's library entitled *Born Crucified*. It was written by L.E. Maxwell, the founder of the Prairie Bible Institute.[3] In it, he explained the difference between being saved from the *penalty of sin* and being saved from the *power of sin* in our daily lives. When God saves us, we are forgiven for all of our sin and the penalty is removed. We are not on probation. We must accept God's work in our daily lives. The cross deals not only with the penalty of sin, but its power. All that we could never be, Christ became for us. Now we purify ourselves, not to get the hope, but because we have it, as 1 John 3:3 promises, "And everyone who thus hopes in him purifies himself as he is pure."

I did not understand all about justification and sanctification, but I now realized sanctification, in the sense of release from the power of sin in our daily lives, was progressive, not instantaneous. I also realized that God did not let go of me every time I sinned. Now the song, "I hold not the Rock, but the Rock holds me,"[4] took on a whole new meaning

In short, as I studied the Scriptures outlined in this book, I was set free. Inside, it said the copyright of this book was MBI. I decided I wanted more such teaching, so I enrolled in the correspondence school of Moody and took several courses. I also wanted to attend MBI as a residential student.

By now, I had decided the Lord might be able to use me in Christian service in spite of my imperfection. Moody Bible Institute seemed a bit radical, as I would be snubbing our own Pentecostal schools, and my father was a top official in the UPC. Instead, I decided to enroll in Bob Jones University in Greenville, South Carolina, a liberal arts college. I was thinking in terms of some form of missionary service.

I was not totally happy once I enrolled at Bob Jones University, especially with their segregation position, and only stayed one year, as I wanted the Bible to be the emphasis of my study. Somehow, I also managed to get through a year in this very strict

---

[3] The Prairie Bible Institute is in Three Hills, Alberta.
[4] Caroline Rice, "Builded on the Rock," 1918.

Bob Jones University, Greenville, South Carolina

school without getting any demerits on my record, so I decided not to risk a second year! Instead, I enrolled in a small Bible institute in Dallas, Texas, for the next school year planning to stay with my brother and his wife, who lived there at the time.

During the first part of August, we were at our annual UPC Camp Meeting at Harvey Lake in New Brunswick. A friend of my father's, Frank Munsey, a pastor in Hammond, Indiana, arrived to meet with my father to discuss missions. We met, and upon learning of my plans, he suggested I go back with him, enroll in MBI and work in his church. He was a very convincing man, and it sounded almost too good to be true. However, I thought I had no chance of getting into Moody at that late date in the summer.

At the admissions office that day in late August, I met the director of admissions, explained my situation, gave him a report card of my last semester at Bob Jones University and asked if there was any chance I might be admitted. He was very kind and was impressed I had made the dean's list at Bob Jones University. He told me there were always some last-minute cancellations and I had a good chance of being admitted. I filled out an application and left.

From there my dad and I went on to St. Louis, Missouri, where I saw the headquarters of the UPC and my father's office

Me and Lelia with Frank and Ruth Munsey.

for the first and only time. Following that, we attended a conference in Little Rock, Arkansas. After the conference, we returned to Hammond, which is close to Chicago. There I learned of my acceptance at Moody. The next day my father left me with Frank Munsey who would take me to Moody when school opened a few days later. Over the next three-and-half years, this pastor would become a dear friend. I am today, his debtor, and owe him more than any man, with the exception of my father.[5] He would take me into his home, his heart and his church. Next to the God who called me, I credit my own ministry to him more than anyone else. Later, when I would consider leaving the Pentecostal ministry, his face would haunt me and I would think of his investment in my life. I did not want to disappoint or hurt him.

---

[5] Phil's mentor was the late Bishop Frank Munsey (1931–2011). Frank's son Steve Munsey took over as pastor from his father and the church, Family Christian Center, in Munster, Indiana, has grown to become a church of over 18,000 members. An interesting *New York Times* article about Frank Munsey and the Family Christian Center can be found at https://www.nytimes.com/2005/07/24/magazine/the-rabbi-who-loved-evangelicals-and-vice-versa.html.

I highly value my years at Moody Bible Institute, as it was there that my Pentecostal foundations were shaken to a point from which I would never recover. I would go on and become a Pentecostal minister, but it would be just a matter of time before I would be a Pentecostal drop-out. Significantly, the shaking of my Pentecostalism would not take place in the classroom. To be sure, the classroom gave me tools of Bible study that would affect my understanding of Scripture, but nothing I was taught in class changed my thinking. A true Pentecostal is a tough nut to crack. Someone has said, "A man with an experience is never at the mercy of a man with an argument."

It was a warm sunny day in September when I arrived at Moody. A returning student helped me get registered and showed me to my room on the eighth floor of the Lawson YMCA nearby.[6] After supper I went to an orientation meeting for new students to hear a challenge from John Phillips. When I returned to my room, I knelt down and thanked the Lord for his leading. I knew I was in God's place for me. I only marvelled at how he had brought it about. In the months ahead, I would say again and again, "My cup runneth over." I enjoyed my student days at Moody more than I ever thought an institution of learning could be enjoyed, but I would graduate as a misfit for the Pentecostal ministry.

My initial days in the Chicago area served to reinforce my Pentecostalism rather than to shake it. First, the church in Hammond introduced me to a new form of Pentecostalism—and I liked it. A number of transplanted Southerners were part of the congregation and brought a warmth I had never before experienced in a church. I could not get over how quickly and graciously they received me. They would invite me to their homes for meals and encourage me to borrow their car or whatever else I needed. It even appeared they enjoyed my pitiful attempts at preaching. The "Amens" were easy to come by and were like "Sic' em!" to a bulldog. Anyone with promise as a preacher could make it in that atmosphere. It was a revved-up form of Pentecostalism with many aspects I would later question, but basically, I felt really at home.

---

[6] Before Culbertson Hall was built, MBI rented the entire eighth floor of Lawson YMCA due to a lack of men's dormitory space on campus.

Moody Bible Institute, Chicago, Illinois

Second, it was in the early 1960s that Pentecostalism crossed the tracks and invaded the mainline denominations. The August 15, 1960, issue of *Time* magazine told about Episcopalians in Van Nuys, California, led by Rector Dennis J. Bennett speaking in tongues. To hear about "God's frozen people" speaking in tongues was something of a bombshell.[7] Before long, other mainline churches were having similar experiences and the modern charismatic movement had launched. Some Pentecostals were skeptical, especially when it reached the Roman Catholic Church, but most of us rejoiced and said, "I told you so." Some friends in the Assemblies of God told me they had hoped for some significant doctrinal changes in their denomination regarding the baptism of the Holy Spirit and the initial evidence of speaking in tongues. However, the outbreak of the charismatic movement confirmed the stand of traditional Pentecostals and removed hope of significant change.

My first encounter with the charismatic movement in a mainline church was in 1962. One of the first churches to have a charismatic group formed was an Episcopal church in Wheaton, Illinois. I heard about it and my curiosity was aroused, so I attended an evening prayer meeting with a couple of friends. The assistant

---

[7] *Time*, Vol. 76, No. 7 (Aug. 15, 1960): 54–55.

pastor conducted the meeting, and it took awhile for me to get used to his clerical collar. It seemed incompatible with someone talking about "the baptism of the Spirit." Two things stood out: first, it was orderly and quiet, none of the loud praying, hand waving or screaming. Second, there was an emphasis on prophecy and not just tongues. When the rector would lay hands on someone and pray, a woman would first say, "spirit of fear," and the rector would say, "Spirit of fear, come out!" Then it might be "spirit of pride" or "spirit of doubt." After the woman prophesied as to the problem, the rector would move to exorcise the spirit. I was fascinated by it all. I was especially impressed when a couple of people requested prayer for deliverance from tobacco. I remembered how troubled I had been to see the Anglican rector in my hometown smoke a pipe. I was sure he could not be a Christian. To see the American counterpart to Anglicans convicted of smoking, convinced me it was indeed a work of the Holy Spirit.

The charismatic movement grew rapidly in America. The Full Gospel Businessmen's Fellowship became a promoter of the charismatic movement in other denominations. Although this organization had traditional Pentecostal roots, they were quick to seize the opportunity. I attended some of their dinner meetings and heard some of the early leaders of the charismatic movement, including Dennis Bennett. I could not afford the meal so I arrived just in time for the speaker.

At the time, MBI was a bastion against Pentecostalism. There were only two Pentecostals enrolled at the time, myself and a young woman. At one time, as a condition for admission, MBI required Pentecostals to sign a statement not to propagate their views. They had not had such problems for some time so I was not required to sign such a statement.

I wondered if the charismatic movement could penetrate MBI. I soon discovered what all institutions and denominations have discovered: you cannot ignore or insulate yourself from the charismatic movement. This is true internationally as well, where the charismatic movement has heavily influenced the global church.[8] One Sunday evening I was free from my church

---

[8] Though maybe not the most current statistics, this June 28, 2017, article by Catholic priest Mathias Thelen communicates the massive influence the charismatic movement

obligations in Hammond, so I attended a Baptist church on the northside of Chicago to hear the editor of *Christian Life* magazine talk about this new movement. I spoke with him afterward, and he told me a student at Moody had received the "baptism of the Spirit," but he did not know his name.

A few weeks later, I received definite confirmation the charismatic movement had penetrated Moody. On another Sunday evening I attended the Philadelphia Church, a Swedish Pentecostal congregation on North Clark Street. To my amazement, I looked over and saw my Hebrew professor. After the service I asked him what he was doing there, and he asked me the same question. Our confessions led to an appointment the next day. This man was a respected Old Testament scholar with his doctorate from Grace Theological Seminary, definitely a non-Pentecostal institution.

We met in his office, and I discovered he had been attracted to the movement when his wife experienced physical healing. She had gone to a charismatic group for prayer, after her own pastor refused to pray for her healing. Later, both had received the gift of tongues. He now believed in a second work, or baptism of the Holy Spirit with tongues as an evidence if not the evidence. Through him, I met a few other students who had received the "baptism of the Holy Spirit," and we had immediate fellowship.

For several months, the number at Moody grew slowly and quietly. At maximum, there would have been a dozen students involved and the one professor. There was no problem as it was not known to the MBI administration. The peace would end during Founder's Week in February 1963. The Full Gospel Businessmen's Fellowship sponsored a meeting in the Lawson YMCA for Moody students. Some of the students involved in the charismatic movement were encouraged to invite their friends. Word spread and it snowballed. The details were not given, just a free breakfast and a speaker. I think perhaps students were attracted by a change in menu for breakfast more than hearing a speaker.

---

has had across a diversity of denominations and why this book still has relevancy: https://www.hprweb.com/2017/06/the-explosive-growth-of-pentecostal-charismatic-christianity-in-the-global-south-and-its-implications-for-catholic-evangelization/. Accessed October 9, 2023.

As I recall, there were thirty to forty students at the first meeting, which doubled for the second meeting.

The speaker was Rev. Harald Bredesen, a Dutch Reformed Minister from New York state. I cornered him in the washroom and warned him to go easy as the students did not know they were there to hear a charismatic speaker. He picked his way along quite carefully and nothing was too objectionable. The success of the meeting encouraged them to schedule a second meeting for the next day. Since I was the only card-carrying Pentecostal, I took it upon myself to help lead the meeting and try to explain what was happening. Word got back to the administration and I was asked to meet with MBI's dean of men the next day, along with another student who had also spoken at the meeting. The charismatic Hebrew professor was also fingered, and he would soon be under fire.

The next morning the meeting was much larger and had not only attracted administration representatives, but also some students hostile to the charismatic movement. At the end of the meeting, those interested in receiving the "baptism of the Spirit" were invited to remain. I had to leave early due to my appointment with the dean so I missed the after-service. At noon, I would learn that about a dozen had received the "baptism" and the gift of tongues.

On my way up the elevator to the dean's office, I discovered that my friend was prepared to give the dean a demonstration of speaking in tongues. I forbade him and urged him to share his testimony, but to let me talk first. I felt I was more experienced in surviving as a Pentecostal in a hostile environment. The dean and his colleagues listened attentively to us. He was understanding, but asked us to cease and desist from any more meetings until there was an official reaction. I was asked whether I had signed a pledge not to propagate my views, to which I answered in the negative. They had looked through my file and could not find one.

I hurried through lunch as I had a long walk to my afternoon job at the Federal Reserve Bank. I worked there in the coin department to put myself through school. At lunch, I briefly saw one of the men who had been at the meeting. He told me about the students receiving the charismatic experience. It would be evening before I would get the details, and it would begin one of the most unsettled periods in my life.

At the after-meeting I had missed, the students wanting the "baptism" were asked to come forward for laying on of hands. They were then instructed to open their mouth, move their tongue and make a noise. When something unintelligible came out, they were pronounced "filled with the Spirit." I felt sick to my stomach. Some of those attending felt it was all fake, and this confirmed it. To make matters worse, a young Episcopal clergyman told some of them that he had a year-and-a-half-old baby who could not speak English, but spoke in tongues. A number of students came armed with their Greek New Testaments. They were told, "We don't know Greek or Hebrew. All we have is our ignorance and experience to stand on." That may have been good enough for them, but not for the Moody students.

To suggest the school was in turmoil would be a gross exaggeration, but news quickly spread and soon most were aware of what had happened. As I talked with the students involved, I found some of them really thought they had spoken in tongues, while others did not know what had happened. Students quickly took sides, with the great majority rejecting the experience. It did cause dissension among friends. Since I had been openly identified with the meeting, I was conscious of strange looks and some of my friends seemed a bit awkward in my presence. However, since I was a very low-profile student, most did not know me. I was very disturbed by the dissension this had caused in the school I had grown to love.

A week later in the president's chapel, Dr. Culbertson addressed the students and faculty on the issue. He was a very gracious, godly man and tried to be conciliatory. However, the bottom line was clear. There was no room at MBI for the charismatic movement. A number in the administration were graduates of Dallas Theological Seminary. They were hardliners, taking the position from 1 Corinthians 13:8 that tongues had ceased with the completion of the New Testament canon. They believed all present occurrences were either "of the flesh" or "of the devil." When I shared my experience with any of them, they were evidently uncomfortable as they listened. Their options as to how to evaluate my experience were very limited.

The pressure was now on my Hebrew professor and friend. Before the end of the year, he resigned. He was one of the finest and most dedicated Christians I have ever met. Never did I detect any bitterness in him. I only got bits and pieces of information, but evidently, he went through a very difficult time. I felt badly that a man like him was lost to the Institute.

What I saw going on forced me to face up to a number of issues that had been troubling me for some time. The charismatic movement tended to divide people between the "haves" and the "have-nots," with the "haves" seeming to feel superior. It troubled me to hear the rejoicing and hand-clapping at a Full Gospel Businessmen's Meeting when another Presbyterian or Baptist was introduced who had received the "baptism." It was almost a political spirit, which rejoices when someone switches parties. I sensed more of a spirit of gloating than really praising the Lord. It seemed an experience was being exalted rather than Jesus Christ. If this were a work of the Holy Spirit, how did it fit with John 16:13–14, where we are told that the Holy Spirit would glorify Christ?

What troubled me the most was this question: *Were we really superior?* As a Pentecostal, we used to say, "Baptists are okay as far as they have gone, but they need more," referring to the baptism of the Holy Spirit and speaking in tongues. My problem was I had begun to doubt our superiority. By now I had had the opportunity to observe these "non-Spirit filled" students for almost two years. Many of them out-prayed, out-witnessed, out-loved, "out-Bibled," "out-everythinged" me and I could not deny it! I was getting fairly well read and could recognize Pentecostal ministers preaching sermons they had taken from books by non-Pentecostal authors. *Why did these Spirit-filled preachers have to get their sermons from non-Spirit-filled men?* It seemed to me the most enlightened and gifted men would be those most controlled by the Holy Spirit. I remember sitting around the table eating pizza with several Pentecostal preachers who were discussing good books by Havner, Tozer, Ravenhill and others, from which to get sermons. I suggested that I knew a good book from which to get sermons, "It's called the Holy Bible!" I was being facetious, but also expressing my concern over the lack of exposition in Pentecostal pulpits. I had been introduced to expository preaching at MBI,

My graduation photo from Moody Bible Institute.

spoiling me for a straight diet of topics.⁹ To me, expository preaching seemed to best fulfil the command in 2 Timothy 4:2, "Preach the word; be ready in season and out of season; reprove, rebuke, and exhort, with complete patience and teaching."

---

[9] Phil loved expository preaching and would go on to write his Doctor of Ministry (DMin) thesis in 1978, at Westminster Theological Seminary, entitled, "Preparation for Exposition with a Biblical-Theological Perspective."

Even the worship I experienced at Moody was better. After I had been weaned from wanting nothing but shallow, lively songs that appealed mainly to the emotions, I found myself enjoying great hymns of the faith. The chapel singing and exposition would stay with me longer than Pentecostal services. I was doubting that we really did have more than these non-Pentecostals.

The question we were asked in the days following the charismatic outbreak was this: "What good will it do us?" One young man who is now a pastor in Long Island, New York, complained to me, "These fellows say speaking in tongues makes you feel good. Kissing a girl makes me feel good. What I want to know is, what good it does you?" I could not answer Les, as I was struggling with this question myself.[10] If I answered, "It gives you power," I would be asked to prove it.

The problem stemmed from the fact that Pentecostals were locked into a rigid position. Speaking in tongues was the initial physical evidence of the baptism of the Holy Spirit and therefore no tongues, no baptism, with no exceptions. I remember as a teenager listening to Billy Graham on his radio show *Hour of Decision* and thinking he must have the baptism of the Holy Spirit. After I attended the 1962 Chicago Crusade, I was sure he must be Spirit-filled, even if my theology would not allow it. I started wondering then if tongues might be *an* evidence rather than *the* evidence.

My confusion in the days following the charismatic involvement at MBI was compounded by the pressure my church in Hammond began to exert upon me. They believed that these Moody students who had supposedly received the baptism of the Holy Spirit needed to be led into the full gospel by being re-baptized in water in Jesus' name for the remission of sins (Acts 2:38), and clean up their lives with proper holiness. The latter was meant primarily for the women, who must let their hair grow and stop wearing make-up, slacks or jewellery. I had long since given up the idea that the effectiveness of water baptism depended on the wording: faith and not the form validated baptism. Even then, baptism was only the confession of saving faith and had no saving effect in itself. I had also ceased being concerned about

---

[10] The "Les" was Les Ayars, as supplied by Doug Blair.

outward appearance such as clothing and make-up. As long as they were "clothed and in their right mind," they were acceptable. As one older preacher put it: "Even an old barn door looks better with a little paint!"

One Saturday evening, my pastor and I had a long and lively exchange on the subject. He told me God had placed me there to bring the full truth to Moody, and I was not doing it. My problem lay in the fact that I was unsure what the full truth really was. I did not sleep well that night. The next day, after the morning service, I went to the pastor and told him I was returning to Chicago and not staying for the evening service. I asked someone to take me to the East Chicago Railway Station where I could catch a train on the South Shore and South Bend Railway back to Chicago. As I stood on the platform that day in late February 1963, I began talking to God and myself. I complained, *How did this happen to me? I used to be so sure of myself and what I believed. I never had any doubts about whether I was in the right church.* I remember how I was so sure of myself, that I would stop on a street corner where a Jehovah's Witness was trying to sell their literature, or some religious group was holding an open-air service. I would stand there appearing interested until someone would come over to talk to me, thinking they had found a "live one." Then, I would hit them both barrels loaded with the "full gospel."

Now, all that self-assurance was gone. My dad said I came out of my year at Bob Jones University as a fighting fundamentalist. I still believed in the infallibility of Scripture, but I was not sure of much else. I continued to complain to myself as I thought of my confusion. I continued to say, *How did this ever happen to me?* Then, all of a sudden it seemed as if God were saying to me, "I did it!" I looked up and saw the wet snow falling, but with my spiritual eyes I saw the sovereignty of God. God was in charge of my life and I had been led by divine providence to the place where I was no longer sure of myself. I guess that is the day I became a Calvinist.[11]

---

[11] A Calvinist is somebody who holds to the views of John Calvin in relation to salvation. Those views include humans are *totally depraved* (thoroughly tainted by sin), humans are *unconditionally elected* by God for salvation, Christ's death was *limited in its effective atonement* for the elect, God's *grace is irresistible* and the *saints will persevere* in their trust in Christ, though Phil taught that the saints' perseverance was more about *God's* perseverance than humans.

3

An identity crisis

"**W**ho am I?" was a question frequently heard in the sixties. We called it the *identity crisis*. Young people were asking, "Who am I?" or "What am I?" in their search for meaning. We have come full circle, and this question of identity once again seems to be on the forefront of everyone's mind. The search for meaning was not my kind of identity crisis—mine was ecclesiastical. In 1963, I was asking myself whether or not I really was a Pentecostal.

After the charismatic outbreak at Moody, my disillusionment with both the charismatic movement and my own Pentecostal heritage began to grow. Aspects of both Pentecostal doctrine and worship had always somewhat bothered me. I had been able to overlook them before, but now they were almost a fixation. On occasion, some of my friends would tell me that I would never make it as a Pentecostal minister. For the first time, I was inclined to agree with them.

Perhaps it was more obvious to others that I was a misfit, than it was to myself. Years later, after I had become a Baptist minister, I was visiting a couple from the church in Hammond, Indiana. I had been the best man at their wedding. During this visit in 1981, they told me about laughing and whispering about me when I would be standing on the platform, stiff as a board, while everyone else was shouting, waving their hands and worshipping. The pastor had come to my defense in my absence, by telling the congregation it was due to my being a Canadian and more reserved.

The noise of Pentecostal worship was only one of my issues. I had begun to wonder whether it was more emotionalism than the Holy Spirit. *Why did it have to be worked up? Why didn't I feel the "blessing"?* I could take the noise and commotion if it were really the moving of the Holy Spirit, but more and more it resembled a hootenanny.[1] Others had begun to notice my "Baptist" tendencies. A couple of years before at a camp meeting, we had one of those services described as "a great service—no preaching." During singing, the front half of the congregation began worshipping, speaking in tongues and dancing in the aisles. It went on for so long that they decided to forego the preaching. I was seated near the front and as the "blessing" fell and more people danced in the aisles, it created a lot of dust from the sawdust and shavings on the floor of the tabernacle. To get away from the dust, I left my seat at the front and went to the back of the tabernacle (I guess, with the other less spiritual ones). A missionary from Colombia who had known me from a child spied me at the back and came all the way back to where I was. "Phil," she said, "You ought to come back to the front and get your soul on fire. You have been hanging around those dead Baptists too long!" I really was not trying to get away from the "fire," only the dust.

Even more disturbing than the worship, were the altar services where people were "prayed through" to the Holy Ghost. They would get around people needing the "baptism" and scream and shake them, sometimes doing this for hours. I actually saw an evangelist, who was holding a revival for us, take hold of the chin of one seeker and shake it to get an unintelligible sound out of

---

[1] An informal folk music party where audience members join in by playing music or dancing and stomping.

him, which could be called "tongues." I remember complaining to the pastor and saying that I thought it was, "as the Spirit gave them utterance" (Acts 2:4), not man.

I look back now and marvel at the patience of my pastor. He should have run me out, as I was questioning nearly everything dear to Pentecostals. Even though we had some heated discussion, during which I would kick every sacred Pentecostal cow, he remained a loyal and true friend. I felt I could trust him enough to let out some of my frustrations.

Disliking Pentecostal-style worship and questioning the cardinal Pentecostal doctrine of tongues as the initial evidence of the baptism of the Holy Spirit, created my identity crisis. The issue I wrestled with in the spring of 1963 was this: *If I can't be a Pentecostal minister, what do I do? Where do I go from here?* It was particularly important, as I would enter my last semester at Moody in the fall. Due to transfer credits, I would be able to graduate in January 1964, and I needed to make some important decisions before then.

I had been involved my whole life with Pentecostal churches—I had no other connections. My first thought was to consider an interdenominational faith mission agency. I had been thinking in terms of missionary service and had enrolled in the mission course at Moody. Frequently, mission representatives came to MBI to meet prospective missionary candidates. Several of these organizations gave me interviews. I considered India, which was one place Canadians could still enter while Americans could not. Friends of mine who were missionaries to India had impressed me with the needs of that land. I could not claim a call, but was open to the Lord's leading.

The mission agency representatives I approached were all sympathetic. They did express varying degrees of concern over my Pentecostal background. Most of their suggestions found a pattern. I was young (and looked even younger). I was single and did not even have a girlfriend (although I had been turned down by some of the nicest girls at MBI). It was suggested I might want to further my education, perhaps two or three years somewhere and then apply to a mission board. By then perhaps, the Lord might have led me to a wife. When I asked one mission agency representative whether his mission board looked negatively upon their male missionaries remaining single, he replied, "No, but our young lady missionaries do!" (The single male missionaries will pull the single female missionaries from their singular devotion to God and his call on their life). I would follow their advice, further my education and try pastoring for a couple of years. In the pastorate, I discovered God's will for my life.

Going to a liberal arts college to get a Bachelor of Arts (BA) degree, which was not offered at Moody in those days, seemed to afford me the best opportunity of getting away from my Pentecostal connections gracefully and perhaps establish new associations. I applied and was accepted at a small Presbyterian college in St. Louis, Missouri, for the spring 1964 term. It would take me about two years to complete my BA. That would put me into new surroundings where I knew no one and perhaps give me a chance to resolve my "identity crisis."

In the summer of 1963, I returned to eastern Canada for the first time in two years. My father was now pastoring a small home missions church (church plant) in Truro, Nova Scotia, and I was to be his assistant that summer. In this way, I could fulfil one of the requirements for graduation from Moody. It would also give me a chance to let my father know of my skepticism and misgivings regarding Pentecostalism.

That summer, I grew closer to my father than I had ever been in my life. Growing up, my dad was away so much engaged in mission work, I really did not get to know him. Even when he came home, he was constantly in and out. That summer, we had long uninterrupted hours to talk.

It was a great surprise to discover my father shared many of my frustrations. Initially, he had found Pentecostalism unattractive, as he felt it was not reverent enough. Seeing people supposedly speak in tongues and yet, showing little or no fruit of the Spirit, had caused him to question the whole tongues-evidence business. He resolved it in his mind in a number of ways. The noisy Pentecostal worship, which he called "clap-trap," was an emotional outlet, but because they were sincere, the Holy Spirit could use it to meet needs. Tongues may not be the only evidence, but he could not say it was not. If some received the "baptism" and did not speak in tongues, they were the exception and the exception only proved the rule. I told him of standing around a

An identity crisis 35

My father, Wynn Stairs, and me.

Pentecostal altar service that resembled a three-ring circus and vowing never to darken the doors of another Pentecostal church. Dad only laughed and told me it was nothing but pride, and if he could get over the embarrassment, so should I. He encouraged me to return to eastern Canada after finishing college, swallow my pride and accept the things I did not like. The Pentecostal movement was where the action was, so I had better be a part of it.

By the time I boarded the train the Saturday before Labour Day, for the long trip back to Chicago, I was in a partial relapse from my decision to leave Pentecostalism. My parents, waving to me from the station platform, reminded me of how hard it is to leave family. The same is true for spiritual family. I would be on the train for three nights with daytime stopovers in Montreal and Toronto. This would afford me ample opportunity to contemplate my future.

The first night I was priest-confessor for a Montreal cab driver who wanted my advice about his much younger girlfriend, with whom he was living (he called it "shacked-up," which was the term then). She was religious and would not marry him until he got a church annulment of his first marriage. But she was willing to live with him. It did not make sense to him, and I was not much help. I did try to share the gospel with him.

The next morning, I was met by a pastor in Montreal who was a long-time family friend. I was to preach for him at both Sunday services, and he would take me back to the train after the evening service. At the evening service, they took up a "love offering" for me that was very generous. The pastor said he thought the "old maids" contributed heavily. By "old maids" he was referring to a few unmarried women in their early twenties. What I did not know at the time was that one of those "old maids" would become my wife! I have never been able to get her to confirm or deny her contribution. She says, what she gave is "between her and the Lord."

During the remainder of the trip, I again felt my identity crisis. My head said I should get out, but my heart told me I could not leave the people who meant so much to me. I arrived back in Chicago early on the Tuesday morning after Labour Day. I had four priorities when I got back to MBI. Having sat up for three nights. The first thing I wanted to do was take a shower and get two or three hours of sleep. Next, I needed to go to the Federal Reserve Bank and get my afternoon job back. After that, I would go to Tad's Steakhouse on State Street for the $1.19 steak dinner (remember, this was 1963!), after three days of eating mainly sandwiches. Finally, I would take the train to Hammond to see my friends there. I did all four things that day.

When I arrived back at the church in Hammond, a meeting was in progress, so a number of people were there. I was greeted very warmly by them, and it hit me afresh of just how much they meant to me. If love covers a multitude of sins,[2] it certainly covers a greater multitude of irritations. That night, I was convinced I would remain a Pentecostal in spite of the irritations.

As my final semester at Moody began, I still planned on going away to study for a BA degree. This would give me a chance to evaluate life outside of the Pentecostal Church. I had taken the opportunity to visit a few non-Pentecostal churches in Chicago. I was impressed with their preaching, but was still enough of a Pentecostal to feel their worship services were "dead." It seemed to me our church in Hammond had much more vitality, and it was not *all* emotionalism. I had witnessed some outstanding conversions. I enjoyed teaching in the church in Hammond, especially in the mid-week services, which were well attended. The people seemed hungry and responsive. Just maybe, a Bible teacher could make it as a Pentecostal minister without having to put on a performance.

My plans to get away from the area by going to a college in St. Louis, were also changed unexpectedly. Occasionally, I would preach at churches in the area, either while their pastor was on vacation, or just to give him a break. One church I had preached in just before returning to Canada for the summer was located in Lockport, Illinois. The pastor, Roger Farley, was interested in education and was attending North Central College in Naperville. He suggested I consider North Central for my BA degree, as it was fully accredited and had a good name. Furthermore, he said, I could live in his home and help him in the church. It was an offer I had to consider.

As I began the fall term at Moody, I applied to North Central and made arrangements in early October for an interview. The registrar actually asked me to help him evaluate my transcripts from Bob Jones University, Moody Bible Institute and some summer studies I had taken at Purdue University. I was generous with myself and received enough transfer credits that I could finish my BA in two semesters, about half the time it would take me at the college in St. Louis. In addition, I discovered I was eligible for a one-third tuition scholarship because my father was a clergyman—North Central College was affiliated with the

---

[2] 1 Peter 4:8.

Roger and Millie Farley

Evangelical United Brethren (now part of the United Methodist Church). The offer I had to consider now became an offer I could not refuse. I saw this as a door opened by the Lord. However, it was also a guarantee I would remain in Pentecostal circles during my college days.

The year 1964 would see me commuting between Lockport and Naperville. Both college and church were different experiences for me. The college was education only and no spiritual help. The speakers at the first two chapel services I attended were

Howard K. Smith of *ABC News*, and Art Buchwald, a humour writer and newspaper columnist. I enjoyed getting to know some of the professors at North Central and their viewpoints frequently challenged my thinking. The college also provided the basis I would need to go on to graduate studies at a later date.

The church was a considerable contrast from the one in Hammond. The church in Hammond was thriving while the one in Lockport was struggling. Pastor Farley did what I think was as good a job as possible, but the church had some built-in problems. After about three years, he started a church in Syracuse, New York, where he would have a fruitful ministry. We had many interesting late-night conversations, as he had an open mind to at least listen to other viewpoints. (He and I were out of touch for about fifteen years until he called me one afternoon. He now serves at an independent church and has moderated his views considerably.) I remain indebted to him, and to a number in the congregation who helped me through college.

The year went by quickly and I finished college just before Christmas. I had to decide what to do next. I found that I could not ignore my dislike of many aspects of Pentecostalism. I was able to suppress most of my feelings, although I still doubted whether I would make it to the finish line as a Pentecostal. I would go to UPC Fellowship meetings, a combined meeting for a number of area UPC churches, and felt out of place. The atmosphere I had experienced at Moody was more to my liking, but I felt captive to my Pentecostal heritage. The only option I could think of was to go on to seminary and then leave the Pentecostals. However, I was growing tired of school and wanted a break.

During this time, I was exposed to Pentecostalism with no respite, except through the radio station WMBI on my daily commute between Lockport and Naperville. There were some painful moments. While studying at Moody, I met a Pentecostal minister who came to MBI to "witness" to the students regarding their need for the "baptism." I was seen as an embarrassment to him. One evening, he was at MBI with a visiting evangelist and I encountered him. The evangelist came down on me pretty hard for not believing the "full gospel." During my year in Lockport, I attended a revival meeting in nearby Joliet, where this same evangelist was preaching. After he had taken care to criticize the women's apparel and make-up, he turned, looked at me and said, "Young man, you who are wanting to straddle the fence, take your ministry and go elsewhere. You will do us more harm than good!" The couple I was with, knew he was referring to me. Afterward, they tried to console me by saying I should just ignore him. But I could not ignore him because I actually thought he might be right.

One evening, I was at a UPC Fellowship that turned into a Pentecostal pep rally. My pastor from Lockport got up and said he was "hopelessly Pentecostal." In spite of my respect for him, I thought, "I hope I am hopelessly nothing!" It was an unpleasant feeling to sense that I had gone too far and become too involved not to go on into the Pentecostal ministry and yet, at the same time, wishing there was some graceful way out. I kept praying for that way out, but none appeared.

On December 17, 1964, I wrote my final college exam and walked out to my packed car in the parking lot. I immediately headed east for the 34 hours of driving that would take me to New Brunswick. By now, my father had returned to pastor the church in St. Stephen, and I was going back home to assist him until I found out what I was to do. I was glad to be finished college and eager to see my folks again, but had serious reservations about whether I was doing the right thing. If I got involved in Pentecostal ministry in New Brunswick near my parents, it would be that much harder for me to leave. If I had realized just how difficult it would be, I might have turned my car in a different direction. The deeper the roots, the more painful the uprooting becomes.

I arrived back at the home where I had grown up at about nine o'clock the next evening, after a long winter drive. My mother and my dog were there waiting for me. Mom told me how our old dog Trix, recognized my footsteps and started wagging his tail. One of the nice things about dogs is that you can change your beliefs and they will still love and accept you!

My home church had changed during the eight years I had been away. The town had experienced economic hard times, forcing a number of people to move away to find work. A number of people had also left the church for other reasons, and it seemed to be suffering from old age. Most of those my age were no longer in the church.

Lelia and I when we were dating.

I would be there most of the time during the next eight months, and do the bulk of the preaching. The people in the church opened their hearts to me, like a boy coming home. My father's return had not been unanimously welcomed, but he had originally written into the church constitution that he was guardian for life, so he could return anytime the pastorate was vacant. I sensed the tension, but they did not seem to hold it against me.

My father wanted me to stay on as his assistant, but I knew the church was too small to support us both. Therefore, I had to look at other options. One option I seriously considered was going out west and affiliating with the Apostolic Church of Pentecost of Canada. This organization was theologically similar to the UPC, except, strangely enough, was Calvinistic in doctrine. In June, I journeyed out to western Canada and preached in some of their churches. Although I thought I would feel more comfortable with this group, a couple of things drew me back east.

Lobster boats, Grand Manan Island

I had preached in a number of the UPC churches in the east during the winter and spring of 1965. While supplying the pulpit for three weeks in Montreal, I got better acquainted with one of the "old maids." The end result would be marriage. I proposed on the second date and married six months later. If a young couple came to my office asking me to marry them under the same circumstances, I would probably run them out. I simply believed God was in it and nearly a quarter century later, I still feel the same way.[3]

I also preached in a little church on an island in the Bay of Fundy. The island, known as Grand Manan, had several small fishing communities on it. One was called Woodward's Cove where this Pentecostal church was located. This assembly was founded by my father as a branch church, when he was in St. Stephen years before. The pastor had been there for fifteen years and wanted to leave. However, because of a split, he did not want to go unless another pastor was ready to come. I enjoyed my weekend there and gave it serious prayer, especially after my three weeks in Montreal.

---

[3] Phil and Lelia were married almost 54 years before he went home to be with his Lord and Saviour Jesus Christ on July 28, 2019.

An identity crisis 43

Our wedding day

I talked with the UPC district superintendent,[4] and he was especially eager for me to go to Grand Manan. He wrote to the pastor who was also very agreeable, and arranged a congregational business meeting with myself and the district superintendent. That meeting on May 13, 1965, was a very unorthodox way to call a pastor. The current pastor got up and said he wanted to leave and felt I was the one to come. The district superintendent who was, and remains, a close friend, said the same thing. The congregation was then asked to raise their hands if they would accept me. All during this time, I was sitting on the platform facing them. The congregation consisted of twelve ladies. Ten of them raised their hands and two abstained. Had it been a secret ballot, I seriously doubt they would have called me. Anyway, the decision was not in my hands, and I would wrestle with it for a month or more before finally accepting the call.

The day after that meeting, I headed back to Illinois via Montreal for graduation. Lelia and I discussed the pros and cons of moving to Grand Manan. I had cold feet about taking the pastorate. The other option was to move to Montreal and get a job

---

4 The UPC District Superintendent was Brother Ed Wickens.

Lelia in front of the parsonage at Woodward's Cove.

there so we could be together. In the end, we decided the Lord wanted us in Woodward's Cove and we should get married later that fall.

On August 30, 1965, I drove my car filled with all my worldly possessions, mainly books, to the pier where it was loaded on a ferry for the trip to Grand Manan Island. My mother went with me for a couple of weeks to help me get going on the housekeeping. The parsonage was furnished, so I needed very little to settle into my new home. The couple who lived next door to the parsonage met us and took us home for supper. They were part of the church family. I would violate something I was taught in Bible college, and that was to not get too close to your parishioners. After we were married, Lelia and I became very close to them. They were dear people, and we would have found it very difficult to survive the two years of isolation on that island without them. Thus, I found myself, though a bit unwilling, a Pentecostal pastor.

4

One of them

A boy once read "God works in mysterious ways, his wonders to perform." He misquoted it saying, "God works in mischievous ways, his wonders to perform." When I accepted the Pentecostal ministry as my destiny and was prepared to be as good a Pentecostal as I could, it almost seemed I had been mischievously placed in a most unusual Pentecostal church. My first pastorate certainly did not fit the Pentecostal mold.

My predecessor had served the church for fifteen years. He had moved there from New Hampshire, and was not of the UPC persuasion. He and his wife shared the preaching and were a very sincere couple. Unfortunately, his wife was the better preacher and on that island of macho fishermen, it turned into a church attended mainly by women. A short time after my arrival, more men were back in attendance.

The church had never been self-supporting, as the pastor had worked at carpentry and masonry on the side. Their method of payment was a bit unusual. The pastor received 75 per cent of the

Sunday offerings. If there were fish, there was money; so the pastor took more than a passing interest in the fishing industry. I told them I would not be working outside the church. If they ate sardines, so would I; if they were eating steak, I wanted to do so also. It worked out well, although the first winter, the only steak we had was deer steak (I had a good hunting season!). Despite this, when we left two years later, we had a new car paid for, no debt and money in the bank. The church has been self-supporting ever since.

Finances were the least of my problems at that first pastorate. My predecessor had been involved in what was known as the Latter Rain Movement.[1] It involved bestowing gifts of the Spirit, especially prophecy. He had taught them to prophesy, but after several years, he encountered a problem. One of the sisters prophesied with the divine attribution, "Thus saith the Lord," and declared it was time for the pastor to leave. He rejected this prophecy, creating confusion, and this eventually led to a split.

The pastor then determined that most of the features of Pentecostalism, such as clapping hands, shouting and praying in unison, would hurt the influence of those who wanted him to leave. Therefore, most of this ceased. Now the worship services and prayer meetings resembled a typical Baptist church. Here I was, trying to be a good Pentecostal minister in a church that was more Baptist than Pentecostal!

On my first Sunday as pastor, I tucked my Scofield Reference Bible under my arm and mounted the platform. It was my intention to give what I thought was the best of both worlds: biblical exposition and Pentecostalism. The first Sunday evening, I preached on the baptism of the Holy Spirit and of speaking in

---

[1] "In the late 1940s and 1950s a movement swept through Pentecostal churches, both Oneness and Trinitarian. This was known as the Latter Rain Outpouring. Later Rain had its birth at North Battleford, Saskatchewan, and also had a strong center in Detroit, Michigan. The emphasis was on the gifts of the Spirit and miracles. The message was to preach love, absolutely no doctrine, and nothing about standards nor holiness. This movement proved to be very devastating for many churches. Assemblies were divided and churches were closed. Most of these assemblies were weak in doctrine. It is a definite fact that churches that were indoctrinated in Truth were not shaken by this spurious manifestation. Instead of destroying the necessity for sound teaching it became a strong proof for the teaching of sound doctrine." See Ralph Reynolds & Joyce Morehouse, *From the Rising of the Sun. A History of the Apostolic Truth Across Canada and the Reflections of a Pioneer Preacher* (Surrey: Conexions, 1998), 156.

tongues. I do not recall preaching about it again afterward. I allowed the prayer meetings with people praying individually rather than in unison to continue for a while. However, I felt their prayer meetings were a drag, so later I tried to get them all praying at the same time like Pentecostals would. It did not work. After we were married and my wife joined me, we decided to take over the prayer meeting and pray like Pentecostals. They sat there (my wife and I knelt), while we stormed heaven for at least a half hour. They patiently waited until we had run out of steam and then one after another, they prayed in their usual way.

I would push Pentecostalism somewhat during the midweek service, but conduct it like a Baptist church on Sunday. The pews began to fill with Baptists. There was unrest in the four Baptist churches on the island, so we had plenty from which to draw. I was repeatedly told I would make a "good Baptist."

Fifteen churches had been built on Grand Manan Island with a population of less than 3,000 people. Almost all were very evangelical, so we had an excellent ministerial group. One day I preached at one of the Baptist churches during a combined service. The next day, an older Baptist minister who was interim pastor at two of the churches came to see me. He told me he appreciated my message and could not believe I was a Pentecostal. When he returned to the mainland, he took it upon himself to make an appointment for me with the general secretary of the Baptist Convention and called me on the telephone to let me know. I was not ready for that, so I never kept the appointment. We did remain friends until his death, and his persistence did influence my later decisions.

I did not know I came across as a Baptist, but evidently my speech betrayed me. I did not come through as a real Pentecostal. One of the church members said to me, "Your wife is a real Pentecostal, but you are not." I could not understand it as I was trying hard to be one. Later, when I was pastoring a Baptist church in the Boston area, one of the area pastors, who previously pastored on Grand Manan Island, told me how he and another colleague discussed how long they thought I would last in the Pentecostal church.

When we would go to UPC Fellowship meetings on the mainland, both myself and our parishioners were out of place. I felt guilty about it because I wanted to make it into a Pentecostal church. As I recall, no one received the gift of tongues during my two years there. The Pentecostal church that had split off from ours called us "dead" and said the congregation was increasing only because we did not take a stand for the "full gospel."

I was torn. On the one hand, I wanted to be a true Pentecostal. On the other hand, I was defensive about our congregation. One could never classify them as "holy rollers" but they were some of the finest Christians I had ever met. The church was very kind to us, and really loved the Lord in their quiet way. I had to ask myself whether there would be any advantage in making them "real" Pentecostals. I decided there would not.

It was not the Pentecostal issue that caused me to leave my first pastorate after only two years, but the isolation. I had lived several years in a big city prior to going there, and I was going stir crazy on that little island. I had committed myself to two years and, at the end of that time, when I received a call to my home church, I was ready to accept. I had considered some other options, such as graduate studies, but felt God wanted us in St. Stephen, New Brunswick.

Summer 1967 was spent in Winona Lake, Indiana. Between pastorates, I attended Winona Lake School of Theology while my wife worked in the office to pay my tuition and our room and board. Winona Lake School of Theology operated in the summer months using professors from leading schools around the United States and England. For a couple of years, it had been affiliated with Fuller Theological Seminary, but now was back on its own. It provided an excellent opportunity for further study, and I enjoyed it immensely. I returned the next summer also.[2]

The school was located next to the Winona Lake Bible Conference grounds so we were able to take in the conference services. During my student days in nearby Chicagoland, I visited the conferences on weekends. I was eager for my wife Lelia to be exposed to the Youth for Christ week and the Bible conferences. We had a great time, and I hated to see the summer end, not just because I

---

[2] Phil wrote his Master of Arts thesis in 1968 at Winona Lake School of Theology entitled, "The Problem of the Formula Used with Water Baptism." It is housed at Bethel University, Indiana.

was enjoying myself so much, but because the prospect of returning to my home church was not very exciting.

The summer at Winona Lake did something else for me. I was back with non-Pentecostal people and involved with non-Pentecostal worship. There, I felt I was back in my element. When I journeyed to Hammond for a couple of weekends to renew acquaintances, I felt out of place. I was very glad to see my friends and introduce my wife to them, but still felt uncomfortable as a Pentecostal. My exit was just a matter of time and opportunity. Nevertheless, I was determined to go back to St. Stephen and give it the old college try.

If there were any place I could "make it" as a Pentecostal minister, it was at St. Stephen. There would be much to hold me. First, the pastor was in total control. I led the church. I appointed the deacons (one year I forgot to have them meet), gave out contracts and could give the church any direction I desired. In addition, it was a moderate church, not given to extremely noisy worship.[3] Unlike Grand Manan, it was a *real* Pentecostal church, but not one that expected a jamboree every service.

Last, but not least, there was the pull of my family. Mother and dad were there, and it was home. I had the companionship of my dad I never knew as a boy. Frequently, we would go fishing or hunting, especially duck hunting. We would visit back and forth on Sunday evenings after church and reinforce each other's prejudices. Years later, dad would write to me near the end of his life and tell me how those years when I was pastor in St. Stephen were the happiest of his life. Leaving home at age nineteen to go to college would be a piece of cake compared to leaving my parents at age twenty-nine to become a Baptist minister.

Immediately upon our arrival in St. Stephen, I poured myself into the work of the pastoral ministry. First, there was the church. I had my father preach a lot of the Sunday mornings for the first year, but I preached every Sunday evening. It soon became our largest service and the one that attracted the most visitors. I pretty well knew my opposition. I made sure I cared for them, especially the older ones. Before long, I had their support. Seeing

---

[3] The church referred to is now called Gateway Cathedral (https://gatewaycathedral.com) and is non-denominational.

My father Wynn T. Stairs

new people, especially younger ones, was an encouragement to everyone. The church had been "in the doldrums" for a long time. In a few months, my initial apprehension was gone and I knew I had not made a mistake in accepting the call to go to my home church.

Me with students I was teaching at United Pentecostal Bible Institute.

I also began travelling to Fredericton two days a week to teach in the United Pentecostal Bible Institute in Marysville.[4] The district superintendent was also the principal of the school, and he was the one who asked me to teach. I taught for three years and found it rewarding. I was somewhat of a rebel, and young people are attracted to a rebel. My response when students pointed out my disagreement with other teachers was not the most tactful. "They are out to lunch" was my favourite, albeit arrogant, reply. Since I was not being paid, I felt free to express myself.

At the annual conference, a number of pastors got up and complained that their young people were not being taught "our message" at the Bible school. Several of the teachers took offense, and offered to resign. They were not the problem. I was not the only culprit, but probably the chief one. Labouring under the delusion that the whole movement could be redirected, I felt I must do my part.

Then there was the UPC Fellowship. We would have regular UPC Fellowship meetings where area churches took turns acting as the host church. Dad loved them and seldom missed one. I also joined in, getting to know all the ministers. The meetings were usually a bit rowdy, but I enjoyed it for a while because I really liked the brethren. Even those who were considered radical I appreciated on a personal level. Their feelings may not have

---

[4] The United Pentecostal Bible Institute is now called Northeast Christian College, and its history can be found at https://www.northeastchristiancollege.com/history.html; accessed November 13, 2023.

been as reciprocal as I thought at the time. They probably felt a bit threatened by me. Frequently they would attack education from the pulpit. Still, they treated me warmly, and I would miss their fellowship when I left. Pentecostals are among the best representatives of the "family of God" feeling. At least that has been my experience.

At any rate, with the church, the UPC Bible Institute and UPC Fellowship meetings, I had a real sense of fulfillment. The first couple of years made me think I would be a Pentecostal for life, particularly due to the blessings at our home church. If I could claim mistreatment by Pentecostals, it would have been much easier to leave. I might be able to concoct a case of unfairness on the basis of some isolated instances, but honesty requires me to give them their due. The Pentecostals are wonderful people, and to this day, I miss their fellowship.

The question then is, what went wrong with such a happy arrangement? While I was affiliated with the UPC, it was with a breakaway district. My father had been instrumental in bringing the church in Maine and New Brunswick into the UPC in 1946. He was the director of foreign missions of the newly formed body. In the merger agreement was a clause that would allow them to break away from the parent body. My father's big political mistake—that cost him his job in 1962—was suggesting the Canadians go back on their own.[5] The churches in the Maritime provinces followed Dad and broke away as of January 1, 1965. They would return a few years later, but I was never affiliated with the international body.

By 1969, it was becoming apparent that most of the pastors regretted the breakaway move; some feared we were compromising. The international group took a much harder line than the Maritime district. That hard line would soon become dominant. At least a third of the preachers had kept credentials with the international body. I sensed the undercurrent within a year or two, and realized my brethren were moving in the opposite direction from what I had hoped. It would not be long before I knew I

---

[5] This move of the UPC Maritime district was not unlike many denominations and mission organizations that have decentralized from the United States and become their own national bodies in recent years.

Superintendent Brother Ed Wickens

was tilting my lance at a windmill in thinking I could be an instrument for a move toward moderation. In the end, the district superintendent, Ed Wickens, who was himself a moderate, urged me to stay and not "desert the ship to the pirates." I countered with, "Even rats know enough to get off a sinking ship." In 1973, the district voted to re-affiliate and a number, including my father and the superintendent, became independent. By that time, I was long gone. I had kept my affiliation for one year after becoming a Baptist minister, but at the end of the year I relinquished my credentials. I am glad I was spared the turmoil that ensued. The warm feelings I have today toward my former brethren would have been harmed had I been part of the dispute.

The year 1968 was the peak of my determination to remain a Pentecostal. Everything pointed in that direction. I was enjoying both the teaching in the UPC Bible School and the fellowship of my brethren. The church was doing well and, unlike Grand Manan, some were receiving the "baptism" by speaking in tongues. We were the strongest evangelical church in town. The main Baptist church was not evangelical, and on Sunday nights, we usually had more people seated in our balcony than they had in their entire congregation.

In the larger scene, the charismatic renewal was in full swing, leaving no denomination untouched. David Wilkerson made a great impact with his book and subsequent movie, *The Cross and the Switchblade*. The Pentecostal and charismatic movement seemed to be where the action was, and I intended to stay a part of it.

Around that time, I had an article published in our denominational magazine entitled, "Why I Am Still Pentecostal" (see Appendix C). I gave the standard reasons: my own experience, the Book of Acts where tongues or its implication is associated with every recorded initial outpouring of the Holy Spirit and just a personal preference—I liked Pentecostal people better. I wrote it to burn those Baptist bridges behind me. A few years ago, when a Pentecostal friend of mine was going through the same conflict, he was intending to write a similar type of article for his denomination. I sent him a copy of that article, plus one I wrote ten years later taking the opposite stand. Perhaps, I suggested, he might not want his thoughts to go to print!

A few events did take place in 1968 that would influence my decision to leave. My wife and I returned to Winona Lake School of Theology for six weeks. Again, I enjoyed it immensely and felt away from the pressure while I was there. When I was away from my Pentecostal environment, it seemed I almost immediately began to question whether tongues was the only evidence and whether we really had so much more than everyone else. The previous year in Hebrew class, one of my fellow students was the pastor of Coral Ridge Presbyterian Church in Fort Lauderdale, Florida.[6] The church was just beginning to make a national impact with its Evangelism Explosion program.[7] The pastor shared with us what was happening in his church. It all sounded like a work of the Holy Spirit— but there was no charismatic element. In fact, the pastor frankly rejected the charismatic movement. On the other hand, the few students with charismatic leanings were an embarrassment to me with their oddball ideas and ways.

A second event would also impact my life. A Presbyterian minister and his wife moved to St. Stephen. He had just graduated from Gordon-Conwell Theological Seminary and was taking up his first pastorate at St. Stephen's Presbyterian Church. As they approached town, he turned their car radio to the local station, WQDY, just across the border in Calais, Maine. They heard some cornpone singing on a religious program sponsored by the local Pentecostal church. Their immediate reaction was, "On no! Is this the kind of religious life this town has?" What they did not know then was that they would become close friends with that very Pentecostal minister they heard on the radio.

Our friendship was immediate and natural. We were about the same age and had the same interests. Almost every day we would be in contact either in person or by phone. He was in a non-evangelical parish and needed encouragement. I found we could have the same "bull sessions" I had so enjoyed at Moody. We were both interested in Calvinism, eschatology and how to make an impact as an evangelical. We shared the latest books and journals.

At first, I tried to interest him in the charismatic movement. Soon, however, he became a catalyst for my misgivings with Pentecostal doctrine and practice. He was the one who finally introduced my name to the West Medford Church where I would soon become pastor. A year later, upon the sudden death of their minister, he would also take over the historic Greenock Presbyterian Church in St. Andrews, New Brunswick.

---

6 The pastor referred to was Dr. James D. Kennedy (1930–2007), former pastor of Coral Ridge Presbyterian Church in Fort Lauderdale, Florida.
7 Evangelism Explosion (https://evangelismexplosion.org) famously asked two questions: 1) Do you know for sure that you will be with God in heaven? 2) If God was going to ask you, "Why should I let you in my heaven?" what would you say?

My relationship with my new friend effected some changes in my thinking. I found I could not defend Pentecostal doctrine with him, and it exposed the chinks in my armour. Later, he had me preach in his churches when he was absent. I donned his Geneva gown and climbed into the pulpit. (It was "climbed," literally, in the Greenock Church as the pulpit was the highest I have ever seen.) I discovered I could function outside Pentecostalism. That Sunday at St. Andrews was the first time I conducted an entire service in a non-Pentecostal church. The people were very receptive. One elder in St. Andrews almost flipped when he found out a "holy roller" had graced their historic pulpit. He had no idea during the service, as I had acted as Presbyterian as they come. After the pastor left to take a church in Schenectady, New York, I was asked to fill the pulpit a Sunday or two in the St. Stephen church. The people did not seem to mind a bit. While all this may sound simple to most, it excited me with the possibilities that might be out there.

The years 1969 and 1970 were my last two years as a Pentecostal. I was living in two worlds. In one, I was still active in my denomination and going full steam ahead in our local church. In 1969, the church voted to relocate and build a new building. In January 1970, the church passed a unanimous motion to incorporate independently if I saw there was a need. By now, the rumblings in my denomination made me think I should protect our local church in case a need to secede developed. I feared the radical part of the denomination would take over. If the church incorporated independently, the denomination could not take our property. I knew the present superintendent would sign the release, but I was fearful of a Pharaoh arising "who knew not Joseph." I did not carry out the motion, but my successor eventually did. Today, the church is independent and does not even have Pentecostal in its name.

One of our favourite songs at the time was, "I'm so glad that I can say, I'm one of them."[8] I still sang it, but I am not sure I meant it. While I continued in my Pentecostal world, I was looking for a way out. I discussed this with my Presbyterian friend. He introduced me to a Baptist minister, a former seminary classmate, who

---

[8] I.G. Martin, "I'm Glad I'm One of Them," 1906.

had been brought up in the Assemblies of God. He was the one who eventually provided an opening into the Baptists.

At the time, I also considered the Christian and Missionary Alliance (CMA). They seemed to have somewhat of a middle ground, believing in healing and a second work of sanctification, but without the tongues or the emotionalism. One evening, after being at a Pentecostal service in another city, I slipped over to the Alliance church where my wife Lelia and I met with the district superintendent of the Eastern Canada region of the CMA. He was a very gracious man and encouraged me to pursue the possibility of ministry with them. Later, I would meet with the New England district superintendent and receive the same encouragement. It never worked out, and I realize now that my ultimate position would be incompatible with the CMA. At that time, however, I still believed in a second work and healing in the atonement.

I went to my father in early 1970, and told him I felt I was in my last year of ministry in St. Stephen. He did not take me seriously. After the Easter Sunday evening service, Lelia and I drove to the Boston area to get in on the giant, annual book sale at Whittemore Associates. Hardcover books were $0.25 and paperbacks were $0.10. Sets of commentaries were $3 to $6. It was a bonanza for students and ministers. We arrived at about 1 in the morning, and I was third or fourth in line. I was even interviewed by the *Boston Globe.* The doors opened at 9 a.m.

We stayed for nearly two weeks with the Reeds in Rhode Island. I had grown up with the husband, David, in the same Pentecostal church, we had graduated from high school together and I had been the best man at his wedding. Now, he was a doctoral student at Boston University and part-time assistant at an Episcopal church in Attleboro, Massachusetts.[9] He and wife lived in an apartment on the top floor of a funeral home in East Providence, Rhode Island, through an arrangement he had with the owners. I do not remember all of our discussions, but I know I went away with a determination to leave the Pentecostals, move to the Boston area, take a non-Pentecostal pastorate and further my education. What I did not know was *when* and *how*.

---

9 David Reed (PhD) went on to become a professor at Wycliffe College, University of Toronto, and is a leading scholar in UPC studies.

Me and David Reed on a tandem bike.

Me and Lelia with Dr. David and Carlynn Reed.

Soon after returning to St. Stephen, we commenced our building program. Lelia and I sold our cottage at the Pentecostal campground and built one on our own property beside a lake a few miles away. It was an opportunity for more privacy, but also to disconnect myself from the Pentecostal camp. I felt a bit guilty about still being so much involved in the Pentecostal movement while also planning to leave. I preached in a morning service at the annual UPC Camp Meeting in 1970. Ten days later I preached in a Baptist church in North Medford, Massachusetts. and met with their pulpit committee.

I had not anticipated leaving for at least a year after building the new church. The opportunity came unexpectedly and prematurely. However, I felt it was my moment of opportunity and I must not let it slip. At the same time, the reality of what I was planning to do hit me hard. I had many moments of wanting to forget the whole thing. There was so much for which to stay. Outside was an uncertain unfamiliar world. The congregation had no idea what I was doing. The best time for me to candidate for a pastoral position was while on vacation. Even after I accepted the call, it would be over two months before I notified the congregation in St. Stephen. Many times I came close to backing out. However, I knew I had to do it. I could no longer live a double life, pretending I was a Pentecostal when I knew I really was not.

5

Why I left

The phone rang late one night while I was pastor of a church in Halifax, Nova Scotia. The voice on the other end queried, "Is this Phil Stairs?" I answered in the affirmative. "Are you the son of Wynn Stairs?" was the next question. Again, I answered in the affirmative. "Did you used to be a United Pentecostal minister?" the inquirer continued. I confessed I had been. Then he told his story of conversion, receiving the "baptism," going to the UPC Bible School and, finally, gave some sordid details of his life. He had been involved in a homosexual relationship with a leader of the Bible school and later with a pastor. I could tell a few drinks had given him the courage to call me. Finally, I asked, "What can I do for you?" He replied, "Tell me this: How could you leave the Pentecostal church?" I refrained from saying, "Because of stories like yours!" I knew he was serious and I tried to treat him seriously. He could not see that something was wrong with his "baptism" of the Holy Spirit.

That question is one I have been frequently asked, "Why did you leave?" It was not that I wanted to leave, from a natural standpoint. The pressure to bite the bullet and remain was almost irresistible. I had always been somewhat of a loner, but I still did not want to displease my family and friends, as they meant a lot to me. There are three reasons I left: a doctrinal, a personal and a professional reason.

First and most importantly, I faced a doctrinal reason. The cardinal Pentecostal doctrine is that speaking in tongues is the initial physical evidence of the baptism of the Holy Spirit. This means that nobody anywhere, since Pentecost, has been filled with the Holy Spirit unless they spoke in tongues. Great missionaries such as Hudson Taylor and great preachers like Spurgeon and Moody were not filled with the Spirit. If this is the case, there would need to be definite scriptural evidence to support something that seems so inconceivable.

That was my struggle. After studying beyond the usual passages in Acts quoted often by Pentecostals, the rest of Scripture does not support the thesis. An elderly Pentecostal minister and a former district superintendent in Ontario wrote to my father a few years before his death. In effect, he wrote that he had been studying the "initial evidence" doctrine, and now, after years as a Pentecostal leader, had some reservations. "Why" he asked, "are tongues not mentioned in the Book of Romans—the most complete treatise on salvation and the Christian life? Why is there no mention of tongues in any of the epistles, except 1 Corinthians? Why cannot a single word be found about tongues in that marvelous book of Hebrews that tells us why Christ is better than Old Testament symbolism? Why is such a vital doctrine as initial evidence not clearly taught in the New Testament?" He finished the letter by saying to my father, "Show this letter to Philip. I hope he doesn't think I have compromised in my old age." What he did not know was that I was asking the very same questions.

In studying the epistles, I noted that frequently and clearly we are told how we know we are saved. The evidence of the Holy Spirit in our life is clearly discussed in Galatians 5:22–26; Ephesians 5:18–20; 1 John 4:2–3, 13–16, but speaking in tongues is not mentioned. The obvious answer of "no" to the question in 1 Corinthians 12:30, "Do all speak with tongues?" troubled me. I could give the standard Pentecostal answer of there being a difference between the *sign* of tongues, which was for all, and the *gift* of tongues for edifying the church, which was limited, but this explanation seemed far-fetched.

In the Book of Acts, I discovered that not every instance of being filled with the Spirit was accompanied by a special manifestation. When Peter defended the conversion of the Gentiles, he pointed out that the Holy Spirit had fallen on them, "as on us at the beginning" (Acts 11:15). The implication seemed to be that this repeat of Pentecost was not a standard procedure when people converted to Christ. The more I studied, the more uncomfortable I became. A doctrine with such enormous importance in Pentecostalism lacked a real exegetical base.

The conclusion left me with a dilemma. How could I continue affiliation with a fellowship that required the acceptance of this doctrine? In my initial applications for ministerial license and ordination, I had indicated my acceptance of the initial evidence doctrine. I had done so, as my father suggested, by saying to myself that I could not prove it was *not* the evidence. I also was affiliated with the Apostolic Church of Pentecost of Canada and every year I had to indicate my continued acceptance of this doctrine to have my credentials renewed. Each year it became more difficult to sign.

As the pressure on my doctrinal integrity increased, I knew eventually I would have to make a choice. I could stay in the Pentecostal movement and affirm the initial evidence doctrine with tongue in cheek (no pun intended) or I could relinquish my credentials and lead my church to become independent. My final option was to quietly leave both denomination and church with as little disturbance as possible. In the end, I would choose the third option, although it would tear me apart.

I also had some personal reasons for desiring to leave. I had not liked Pentecostal-style worship. It had far too much emphasis on emotions. While I know that emotion plays an important part in any intimate relationship, and none is more intimate than our relationship to God. However, when emotion becomes dominant, feeling supersedes faith. In my Pentecostal circles, emotion was dominant. Without a lot of whooping and hollering, the service was "dead." With the noise was the report, "The Spirit really blessed us" or "We had a great service."

Some will accuse me of an unfair generalization when I say the most emotionally demonstrative people were also the most unstable and inconsistent ones. Other pastors shared the same admission in their more candid moments. I saw far more stability and consistency in quiet Christians, whether Pentecostal or non-Pentecostal. It made sense, because those who only wanted "the blessing" did not seem to appreciate Bible teaching and exposition. It also made sense, because those capable of emotional highs are also capable of emotional lows. It was what Vance Havner called, "Malaria religion—first a fever, then a chill."

One of the side effects of the emphasis on feelings is an extremely high casualty rate. I would hear of great revivals where dozens were saved and "baptized" in the Spirit. Frequently, even before the evangelist left town, many were already backslidden. One neighbouring pastor told me that of the thirty-three receiving the "baptism" in a recent "revival," not one stayed in the church. It was a personal aggravation to me that our church was called "dead" because we did not have the commotion, even though our church was steadily growing and we were keeping those we gained. Now, I know that our Lord lost one of twelve,[1] but something is radically wrong when it is eleven out of twelve.

My personal conviction was that the problem was twofold. First, legalism made staying in the faith a matter of *works* rather than *grace*. Second, equating an emotional outburst with the "moving of the Spirit" was problematic. A stable Christian life is not produced by jumping from one emotional high to another.

The emphasis on feeling would not go away—spirituality and noise are wed in the Pentecostal movement. The charismatic movement has developed a quieter form of worship, but it has the same emphasis on feeling over doctrine and holy living. I felt this frustration every time I attended a UPC Fellowship or camp meeting. Such meetings had to have the "blessing," by whatever means. Everything would be engineered to work people up.

Once, I took our young son to a Pentecostal camp meeting. The band, complete with drums and synthesizers, was louder and livelier than any I remember. After we left, he said, "Daddy,

---

[1] This is a reference to Jesus' one-time follower, Judas Iscariot, who betrayed Jesus (Matthew 26:47–49).

how come you brought me here since you don't want me listening to rock music?" It is no coincidence that the late king of rock and roll, Elvis Presley, was brought up Pentecostal. As secular rock and roll becomes more intense, so has its Christian counterpart. Some Pentecostals say modern rock and roll is the devil's counterfeit. They may want to question who is copying whom.

Compounding the problem of feeling out of place in Pentecostal worship was that I felt so comfortable in non-Pentecostal worship. I was getting the nickname of "the Baptist" and gradually the message got through to me. My place was not with Pentecostals. If I were closer to Baptist doctrine and more comfortable in Baptist worship, why not switch? I was delayed in my switch because of a hearty dislike for Baptists. I had some unpleasant experiences with a few fundamentalist Baptists, telling them they were "so narrow-minded, they had only one eyebrow." It was the denominational pride in some who said "I'm a Baptist" with great feeling, that I disliked in Pentecostals. Eventually, I would have to become in name what I was in spirit.

An additional reason for leaving Pentecostalism was professional. I frequently felt more like a performer and manipulator than a pastor and teacher. There was tremendous pressure to give in to those who wanted emotion and excitement at every service. Pentecostal pastors must be cheerleaders to work the crowd up. That definitely was not my niche.

We did not get a lot of pressure from our local people, who I call the "natives." It was mainly the "imports," people who had moved in from other Pentecostal churches, who gave me the most problems. No matter how well our church was doing in terms of growth, they wanted the "blessing." There was no "liberty" in our church, they would say. In most cases, I knew the church they came from was in constant turmoil, always bickering over something. Their previous church had the "freedom of worship" and now they felt stifled.

Once in a while, I would capitulate and give them what they wanted. It was quite simple. I would start by having the congregation sing some fast and lively choruses. Next, I would have them stand and switch into a slow song like, "He Touched Me" or "Only Believe." Then I would tell them to sing it again with eyes closed and their hands raised. It seldom failed. Someone would give a message in "tongues." Others would join in crying or praying loudly. Soon the majority would be "worshipping" Pentecostal-style. People would be delighted and tell me how much they "felt the Spirit" in the service. I did not know how much the Lord used that type of thing and how much was sheer manipulation of peoples' emotions. What I did know for sure was it left me with an uncomfortable feeling.

Pentecostals do not realize just how much crowd manipulation takes place in their circles. I am not suggesting manipulation is the sole domain of Pentecostal preachers. I have watched Baptist evangelists give invitations, which made Pentecostals look like amateurs when it comes to emotional pressure. However, the tendency toward manipulation is more a part of Pentecostal worship and preaching.

I watched visiting preachers intentionally working up people through music, their preaching or in the altar service. What I found hard to take, was the fact that people gobbled it up. My feelings of repulsion came to a head during my last year as a Pentecostal pastor. A family from Scotland was touring our area. I was urged to have them come minister at our church as they were reported to be the most "spiritual" group around. Some of our people who had heard them in other churches urged me to have them as they had "never heard anyone like them." So I had them for several evening meetings. They sang choruses they had written and taught to the people. They were real winners. The crowds came and the altar was filled. Every service had "the blessing." They had the people in the palms of their hands.

The group was primarily a family, and the parents stayed in our home. When my wife and I cleaned their bedroom, I noticed a number of books on the dresser. Being a bookworm, I was interested in what they were reading. Aside from Alexander Whyte's *Bible Characters*, the rest were all about performance. I wrote down the titles: *The Magic Power of Emotional Appeal* by Roy Garn, *Make More Friends—The Key to Success* by Gilbert Oakley, *How to Sell Yourselves to Others* by Elmer Wheeler, *Rhetoric for Exposition* by Roger Chittick and Robert David Slevick, *Perfect Everything* by J. Rufus Moseley and *How to Use Tact and Skill in Handling People* by Paul Parker. They may have had other books with them in their car or suitcases, but those were the ones they had out.

I am not suggesting this family group were phonies. Since they were new to North America, they probably felt pressure to perform well in order to get established. If that was the case, it worked because I see them on television every so often. I just found it very hard to listen to them talk about depending totally on the Holy Spirit when I knew they were using human manipulation techniques. The group's leader even preached from Zechariah 4:6, "Not by might nor by power, but by my Spirit saith the Lord."

While few would admit it, Pentecostals have tended to equate the working of the Holy Spirit with certain emotional feelings and responses. That makes them susceptible to a good performer. Because they are looking for a quick fix through an emotional release, they can be fairly easily taken in by a phoney.

In 1971, a movie entitled *Marjoe* created a stir.[2] It was about a former child evangelist, Marjoe Gortner, who took a film crew around with him just before he left the preaching circuit to pursue a Hollywood career. He freely admitted he never believed anything he preached. He was taught how to preach as a little boy by his parents, and he learned how to manipulate a crowd. He could speak in tongues, lay hands on people and have them fall over "under the power." He would then take the offering, leave the tent to go to a motel and spend the night with a girl or head for the disco.

I attended one showing with an Irish preacher friend of mine, then a Pentecostal pastor in Bangor, Maine, who has since made it on TV.[3] He groaned as he watched Marjoe put it over on some of his personal friends in the field of evangelism. I have always prided myself on being able to spot a phoney, but I think, just maybe, Marjoe could have fooled me. He was that good.

Pentecostal people will respond, "It doesn't matter about the vessel, God honours his Word." However, that fails to adequately

---

[2] More information on the movie *Marjoe* can be found at https://www.imdb.com/title/tt0068924/.
[3] The preacher was the Bob Gass (1944–2019) who became an author with United Christian Broadcasters.

address the facts. A lot goes on in Pentecostal meetings that has nothing to do with the Holy Spirit. A good performer can give people what they want if they are willing to settle for noise and an emotional feeling. When I watched the movie *Marjoe*, a few months after I left the Pentecostals, I had two reactions: 1) I was glad I had left; and 2) I wished every Pentecostal would watch it.

I found it very disturbing to see that Marjoe Gortner duped so many. He had all the Pentecostal grimaces and groans down pat. He could look upward with such a spiritual expression on his face that one thought he could see heaven. There was a refreshing humility about him. I left that theatre in Brighton, Massachusetts, shaken. It hardly seemed possible that someone could seem so real and yet be as phoney as a three-dollar bill. It is very possible to say all the right things, go through all the right motions, get all the desired "results" and yet not know God.

Pentecostals have developed an emotional type of worship that must be maintained at any cost. Inevitably, when the "blessing" falls in a service, people begin to speak in "tongues" together. This is in direct violation of 1 Corinthians 14:23, "If, therefore, the whole church comes together and all speak in tongues, and outsiders or unbelievers enter, will they not say that you are out of your minds?" Yes, they will, and they do. Many an outsider has gone into a Pentecostal church and thought they were crazy. 1 Corinthians 14:27–28 is violated every Sunday in Pentecostal churches across the globe, but the pressure to perform causes preachers to ignore it or give some ridiculous explanation to these verses.[4] Frequently, in their welcome package for visitors, Pentecostal churches include explanations for things that might scare new people who are not familiar with their style of worship.

Pressure to perform is carried into the after-services, where people are prayed through to the "baptism." As the pastor and primary worship leader, I found this very hard to handle. Fortunately, I had a few dear souls who would do it for me. They would stay by the person needing the "baptism" and exhort them to "hang on" or "let go," whichever they thought was appropriate.

---

[4] "If any speak in a tongue, let there be only two or at most three, and each in turn, and let someone interpret. But if there is no one to interpret, let each of them keep silent in church and speak to himself and to God."

They would urge the person to pray louder or faster, to speak it out and if need be, they would help these people. They are dear sincere people who only want to help others receive what they think they need. However, when I watched them, and as a Pentecostal preacher, I had a responsibility to wander through the prayer room and give encouragement. I would ask myself, "Does Acts 2:4 teach that the Spirit gives the utterance, or does the utterance give the Spirit?"

This became one of my main complaints. It seemed to me that Pentecostals had things backward. *Do you shout to get joy or because you already have it? Is praise to put something into your heart or the outgrowth of something already there?* I strongly believe emotion is an integral part of our relationship to God, but emotion is always a *result* and not a *cause* of intimacy to God. Some examples come to mind. There is sorrow because we have sinned against a holy God. There is awe because we have come to understand the majesty of God. There is joy because we appreciate the grace of God. I am not even against an outward manifestation of emotion. I am simply against trying to work up emotions by visible manifestations or lively music to *create* the "joy" or "sorrow."

The need to speak in tongues as evidence of the Spirit's baptism has become so central to Pentecostals that they will do almost anything to induce it.[5] Now, training courses exist to help you speak in tongues (see Appendix A). Apart from the simple laying on of hands, I could find absolutely nothing in the Book of Acts to justify trying to induce the Holy Spirit to come upon someone. According to Galatians 3:2, the Holy Spirit comes when we hear and believe. We do not have to beg him to come.

The longer I remained a Pentecostal, the more my professional ethics were at stake. *Could I perform what people wanted even though I did not believe it was scriptural?* Should I turn the church away from mainstream Pentecostalism and become independent? If I did that, I would eventually have a split. Up to this point, I had successfully kept everyone somewhat happy, at least happy

---

5 Since the time of writing, Pentecostalism has undergone changes including some Pentecostal denominations no longer requiring speaking in tongues as the evidence of salvation and baptism of the Holy Spirit. For a quick overview of these changes and a critique, check out: https://www.thegospelcoalition.org/essay/pentecostal-theology/. Accessed October 14, 2023.

enough so all voted for me to remain as pastor. However, I had done so by smothering my personal convictions. I was increasingly convinced we were on the wrong track. I would choose a new train, rather than getting my church to switch tracks. A few years after I left, the church did have a split and the more extreme Pentecostals left, starting their own church. It was probably the best for both sides.

For the first couple of years when my wife and I would meet former colleagues, they would frequently ask how we felt about being out of the Pentecostal church. Our standard answer was, "Relieved!" The pressure was off. I do not know how other Pentecostal ministers handle the pressure to perform. Some seem to thrive under it. With me, the pressure became so intense that I became willing to leave family and friends, be the object of scorn and become part of the one denomination for which I had frequently expressed a personal dislike.

Ministry itself changed very little for me after I switched denominations. My pulpit ministry had always been the exposition of Scripture, usually taking a book of the Bible and going through it verse by verse. That has not changed. The pastoral care aspect of my ministry changed little as well. What really changed was I no longer felt I must be a performer.

6

Is this that?

An elderly Pentecostal minister whom we all loved, pastored in a fishing village near us for many, many years. When he really got warmed up preaching, he would say, "This is that and that is this. If this isn't that and that isn't this, what's this and where's that?" He was referring to Acts 2:16 where Peter explained what had happened on the Day of Pentecost by saying, "But this is that which was spoken through the prophet Joel." We would sing:

Brother, this is that,
Sister, this is that,
This is that, that fell at Pentecost.

Pentecostals maintain they have recovered what the New Testament church had on the Day of Pentecost and in the Book of Acts, namely, speaking in tongues, healing and miracles. A question I had to confront—and I think all charismatics and

Pentecostals should face—is, "Is this really that?" Do we actually have today what is recorded in the Book of Acts? My response is: "No, we do not have today what took place in the New Testament."

There was a time when I would have considered the above statement the rankest of heresy and evidence of a closed mind. I could have given names and places to prove we have what is recorded in the Book of Acts. However, a closer study of the New Testament, and a survey I have taken over the years, have convinced me, this is not that. My survey is not scientific, but I think it would stand up under scrutiny. I have asked dozens of Pentecostal ministers this question, "How many miraculous healings can you attest to personally that involve congenital blindness, paraplegics or raising the clinically dead?" The answers always have been, "Very few or none." With open honest minds, let us look at the issues and ask a few questions.

Regarding speaking in tongues, on the Day of Pentecost speaking in tongues definitely meant speaking in *actual* languages:

> And at this sound the multitude came together, and they were bewildered, because each one was hearing them speak in his own language. And they were amazed and astonished, saying, "Are not all these who are speaking Galileans? And how is it that we hear, each of us in his own native language? Parthians and Medes and Elamites and residents of Mesopotamia, Judea and Cappadocia, Pontus and Asia, Phrygia and Pamphylia, Egypt and the parts of Libya belonging to Cyrene, and visitors from Rome, both Jews and proselytes, Cretans and Arabians—we hear them telling in our own tongues the mighty works of God" (Acts 2:6–11).

There is no reason to understand tongues in the rest of Acts and in 1 Corinthians to be anything else but actual languages. 1 Corinthians 13:1 may also allow the language of angels, but that is another issue. There is no exegetical basis for understanding the meaning of *tongues* as gibberish and not a language. All biblical speaking in tongues should involve an actual language the speaker has not learned.

Statistics numbered charismatics and Pentecostals worldwide as high as 270 million in 1987, and 644 million in 2020.[1] With several public services a week, fifty-two weeks a year, it is not unreasonable to speculate there may be more than 1 billion utterances of speaking in tongues each year in these circles. Certainly no one could question a figure in the millions. Allowing for half to be the language of angels, and another quarter to be dead languages or dialects not yet identified, there still should be millions of public utterances in *known* languages.

Here is my question: If this is that—what they had at Pentecost—where are the recordings of people speaking in tongues which can be identified by language experts? I have not heard of any. If the modern tongues movement is really languages, like Acts 2, the sheer numbers of charismatics and Pentecostals would mean we should have numerous identifiable recordings. The fact is, we do not. I have frequently thrown out this challenge with no response. Well, it usually evokes some animated responses, but no recordings. Attempts have been made to record speaking in tongues to determine whether or not they are actual languages. None are what could be called an exhaustive, scientific survey. However, the results are interesting.

A sympathetic researcher and writer, John Sherrill, said that his language experts could not identify his recordings as known languages, but that they did have *characteristics* of languages.[2] A non-sympathetic, but probably objective researcher, maintains that modern glossolalia (speaking in tongues) is linguistic nonsense. In an article excerpted from his book and printed in *Psychology Today*, he suggests the similarities to real languages are only because the speaker unconsciously wants it to resemble a language.[3] Over several years of study and visiting numerous tongues-speaking groups in different countries, he concluded that glossolalia is not a language, but nonsense syllables.

---

[1] Julia Duin, "The Holy Spirit and World Evangelization," *Christianity Today* (September 4, 1987): 45. According to a 2020 study, the number of charismatics and Pentecostals in the world is 644 million (https://brill.com/view/journals/pneu/42/3-4/article-p327_1.xml?language=en). Accessed October 15, 2023.
[2] John L. Sherrill, *They Speak with Other Tongues* (New York: Pyramid, 1964), 100.
[3] William J. Samarin, "Glossolalia," *Psychology Today* (August 1982): 48ff.

These studies do not create or destroy faith in glossolalia, but they do raise an important question for Pentecostals. If we have a modern Pentecost, why can it not be readily proved to the skeptical, as it was on the Day of Pentecost? Taking even the most conservative estimate of 15 million charismatics and Pentecostals in North America, and with speaking in tongues on national TV weekly, why do we not have recorded proof that modern tongues-speaking involves actual languages? To me, the unavoidable answer is, with a few possible exceptions, the modern tongues movement does not involve real languages.

Turning to the subject of healing, the same questions must be asked: *Do we have healings today like those recorded in the New Testament?* Two areas of evaluation are needed: quantity and quality. First, quantity: *How many were healed in the New Testament?* There were occasions in the ministry of Christ where many sick people were brought and he healed "every one of them" (Matthew 8:16; 9:35; 12:15). The same happened during the ministry of the apostles (Acts 5:16; 10:38). That is not to say that everyone in the country was healed. Rather, in a particular meeting, with a large number of sick present, the success rate was 100 per cent. Nothing remotely similar happens today. In healing meetings, with a large number of sick present, only a small percentage at best will even claim to be healed. No healing campaign comes close to even a 50 per cent success rate. No one today claims to occasionally empty a hospital. Yet the equivalent took place during the ministries of Christ and the apostles.

Second, in the quality of healing, we also notice a difference. The Gospels and Acts record healings of congenital blindness and paraplegia, and even raising the dead (John 9:1; Acts 3:2; 9:40). Today, how many people who were blind from birth have been instantly healed? What about paraplegics? Are any funeral processions being interrupted in order to raise the dead? Instead, it is usually the things that cannot be verified, such as headaches, pains, stiffness and so on. I have yet to meet someone who can give me the name and address of someone blind from birth who has been healed, and the name and address of the doctor who verified it. It is obvious from the ministry of Christ that his healings were verified. His *enemies* even talked about putting Lazarus to death because so many skeptics were "believing in Jesus" (John

12:10–11). I have not heard of skeptics being convinced by faith healers today.

What I have just written sounds like the words of the typical cynic. The fact is, I am not a skeptic, but a believer. I believe God *can* and *does* heal today. I know of at least two cancer patients who were completely healed after they had been given no hope by doctors. I remember in a church I pastored, a woman quit her insulin shots after prayer and lived for years without them, finally dying of an unrelated disease. I believe that had a video camera been present when I was nine, it would have actually recorded a language spoken in Liberia, Africa. I also believe that this has happened to others. I even believe that if someone would adequately fund a research project, evidence of miraculous healings and legitimate speaking in tongues would be found. However, I am confident they would be the rare exception and not the rule.

What I am trying to say is: *This is not that*. We do not have the same manifestations of healings, miracles and tongues that were present in the New Testament. They may exist today, but they are certainly not a normal or commonplace part of the church. Pentecostals need to honestly face the facts. Unless they can produce emptied hospitals, interrupted funeral processions and recordings of people speaking unlearned languages, then this is not that.

We are then left with two questions: *What is this? Where is that?* The last question first: *Where is that?* Did God intend for signs and miracles to be a normal part of church experience? The answer has to be "No," or God has failed. To attribute the cause to our unbelief does not deal with all the facts. Frequently, God did work in the presence of unbelief as with Pharaoh (Exodus 7:8–13). Man cannot frustrate God's overall plan or man would be sovereign, not God.

The whole question of miracles and signs goes deeper than that. A number of scholars, including John R.W. Stott, have noted that signs and miracles are not found uniformly throughout biblical history. Instead, they appeared primarily, although not exclusively, in clusters. These clusters are found around the ministry of Moses, Elijah and Elisha, Christ and the apostolic church. A closer look reveals these to be major epochs of revelation, denoting a definite movement in the history of redemption.

Moses marked the giving of the Law. Elijah and Elisha marked the beginning of the prophetic ministry, calling for judgement of the old Israel. The ministry of Christ and the apostles revolves around the central redemptive events of the cross and the resurrection. At each point, *miracles and signs served to authenticate God's redemptive activity*. Hebrews 2:3–4 bears this out regarding the ministry of the apostles ("it was attested to us by those who heard"). Beginning in Genesis and continuing through Revelation, signs and miracles were not a continuous or normative part of God's dealings with his people. The church continues this pattern, as shown by the lack of emphasis on signs and miracles in the teaching epistles of the New Testament. It is true there were exceptions to the cluster rule of miracles in the Bible, and undoubtedly there are exceptions today. The point is, signs and miracles are not a *normal* part of church life today. The reason is not a lack of faith, but simply God's sovereign dealings with his people.

The next major event in the history of redemption is the second coming of Christ. A case might be made for expecting miracles to precede the second coming of Christ, as they did during the Exodus. If there is an increase in authentic miracles today, it might point to the imminent return of Christ. However, a note of caution should be sounded. Miracles did not precede his first advent. Instead, they followed Jesus' coming in the same way the miracles God did under Moses later on in his life, as was in the case of Elijah and Elisha. In addition, the signs listed in Matthew 24 regarding Christ's second coming do not include miracles.

At this point, it might be appropriate to discuss the issue of divine healing. Some more radical Pentecostals distinguish between *divine* healing and *medical* healing. However, should not *all* healing be considered divine healing, as it ultimately comes from God? Medical personnel do not invent or create cures, they *discover* them. God has created these cures. It is inconsistent at meal time, to thank God for "his provision" and accept the human element from farmer to cook, while refusing to accept the human element in God's provision for healing. All medical healing *is* divine healing. It is certainly not a lack of faith to go to a doctor. On occasion, God may bypass doctors, just as he bypassed any human element in providing food for Elijah (1 Kings 17:4), but it is the exception, not the rule. God has provided for both sustenance and healing using human means. We should thank God for medical "discoveries."

Fair questions to ask are: *Do Pentecostals have better health due to faith healing? Should they not live healthier and longer lives?* My contention is that they do not, at least not significantly. Studies have shown that Seventh Day Adventists live longer and have less incidences of certain diseases due to their vegetarianism. However, I know of no studies that show Pentecostals are healthier or live longer. As a Pentecostal pastor, I had to visit the hospital as frequently as I do now as a Baptist. Possibly, some healings stem from the fact Pentecostals seek for healing and request it more than others. Again, it is the exception and not the rule. Baptists tend to pray for God to use doctors and medicine, but both pray for the sick.

A purely subjective view would be that Pentecostals seem to be more open to the Lord's leading and this may lead to healing in an indirect way. Years ago, my wife had surgery for a thyroid condition. That next Sunday evening, a woman handed me an envelope and said, "The Lord impressed me to give you this." Inside the envelope was $200. At that time, it was a considerable sum and would equal my salary for two weeks. The next day I went to the post office and received the surgeon's bill, which came to exactly $200. On the way out of the post office, I met the woman who had given me the money. I showed her the bill, and I know it made an impact on both of us. Now, the Lord could have simply prevented or cured my wife's thyroid condition directly. I happen to believe he used a doctor with skill and a Pentecostal woman with means, to supply the need. God did multiple things at once. He increased the woman's faith, generosity and listening skills for his voice, healed my wife, encouraged my faith and provided for the doctor's family and staff through this indirect healing—that may not have happened with a direct healing. It may never convince an atheist of the existence of God, but it was a blessing to me.

The question regarding speaking in tongues and Pentecostals is more complicated. *If this isn't that, what is it?* First of all, I want to eliminate the suggestion that it is of satanic origin. It would be difficult to find more sincere Christ-loving people than Pentecostals, and few who more diligently seek God than Pentecostals.

To suggest God would allow Satan to take over their life is entirely inconsistent with Luke 11:11–13.[4] While any group is open to the attacks of the enemy, I do not believe tongues are induced by demons. If they were, it would be real languages, as Satan's counterfeit would be a copy of the real thing.

That leaves me with only one very uncomfortable option. They must be emotionally and psychologically induced. Again, I do believe there are incidences where God gives a real language, but they must be rare or we would have more evidence. The mind is a strange thing, and lots of times it can produce what it wants to produce. I am convinced this happens to Pentecostals or charismatics desiring to speak in tongues.

What I cannot answer is how much God uses this as a means of worship. There are aspects of our worship—from the sound system to musical instruments—that are not found in Scripture. Yet, I believe God can use these things to enhance worship. Some cultures have very different forms of worship from what I could enjoy, but I accept their validity. I would take the approach that if it does not produce evil results, and if it is not forbidden in Scripture, then we have no right to condemn it.[5] Some may be helped in worship by hand-clapping, arm waving, boisterous singing, dancing in the aisles, shouting or using "ecstatic speech." Frankly, I do not feel comfortable with it, but I am not prepared to condemn it.

What I am trying to say is that God may use "ecstatic speech," for want of a better term, in worship. It may not be wrong, but I do not believe it has a scriptural basis. The biggest problem arises when it gets out of control. Those who claim that, when the "Spirit moves," they have no control and must burst out in tongues or prophecy, are totally in violation of Scripture. 1 Corinthians 14:27–32 clearly states that tongues and prophecy are completely under the control of the speaker. An outburst in a worship service is due to uncontrolled emotions and not the Holy Spirit.

---

[4] "What father among you, if his son asks for a fish, will instead of a fish give him a serpent; or if he asks for an egg, will give him a scorpion? If you then, who are evil, know how to give good gifts to your children, how much more will the heavenly Father give the Holy Spirit to those who ask him!"

[5] Phil held to the normative rather than the regulative principle of spiritual experiences. The *regulative principle* holds that one will only do what is *found* in Scripture. The *normative principle* holds that one will do whatever is *not forbidden* in Scripture.

Emmanuel Baptist Church, Chatham, Ontario

In our church,⁶ I do not encourage hand-clapping, raising of hands and closing one's eyes while singing, or any of the other aspects of worship that set Pentecostals apart.⁷ I do not believe they are wrong. I am concerned what they will lead to. A charismatic is the type of person who would be encouraged by this to take over a service with prophecy or speaking in tongues. This very thing happened in a nearby Baptist church, with disastrous results. We have a number of Pentecostals or Pentecostal-related people in our church. They are some of our finest members. I know they are with us because they want to be. If they wanted Pentecostal-type worship, they could go to a very fine and respected Pentecostal church nearby. I would introduce them to

---

⁶ Phil was the senior pastor of Emmanuel Baptist Church in Chatham, Ontario, Canada, at the time of writing.
⁷ Since the time of writing, these expressions of worship have become more mainstream evangelical and find merit in the Scriptures, such as the apostle Paul's encouragement for "men should pray, lifting holy hands" (1 Timothy 2:8).

the pastor, who is a close personal friend, and wish them well.[8] The type of expression that is accepted in one church may cause division in another.

The exuberance of Pentecostal worship has a wide appeal, particularly to young people. The music is more to their liking. Frequently, the preacher is more entertaining than a simple expositor. One day when my daughter was about five years old, I had her on my knee and asked, "Who is your favourite preacher?" Her response was, "Jimmy Swaggert!" My kids know how to keep me humble! Sometimes I am surprised that Pentecostals have not made more inroads into other churches than they have. A quicker response can be generated from the emotions than the intellect. While I believe God can and does use the emotions, they should not be confused with the Holy Spirit.

The argument frequently used by Pentecostals is that signs and miracles are needed to convince the unsaved of the reality of the gospel.[9] Jesus condemned this type of thinking in the strongest possible terms by saying, "An evil and adulterous generation seeks for a sign, but no sign will be given to it except the sign of the prophet Jonah" (Matthew 12:39). The preaching of the resurrected Christ is the basis of faith. The only miracles that become the foundation of faith are the miracles of Christ recorded in Scripture (John 20:30–31).

When Jesus spoke about the rich man and Lazarus in Luke 16:19–31, he gave us an important truth. When the rich man requested that Lazarus return to warn his brothers, he was told, "They have Moses and the Prophets; let them hear them" (in other words, Scripture). The response was that Scripture is not enough, they need something spectacular like an opened grave. The reply is simple: "If they do not hear Moses and the Prophets, neither will they be convinced if someone should rise from the dead." In other words, if people are not brought to repentance through hearing Scripture, nothing can save them.

---

[8] The close friend and pastor of the local Pentecostal church, Evangel, was Wayne Dawes (PhD).
[9] Those arguing that tongues is a witness to unbelievers may cite 1 Corinthians 14:22, "Thus tongues are a sign not for believers but for unbelievers, while prophecy is a sign not for unbelievers but for believers." The apostle Paul was most likely referring to unbelieving Jews since he quotes Isaiah 28:11–12 in the preceding verse.

Those who call for a "miracle ministry," in order to have an impact on the world, are following the thinking of the rich man in Hades. Spectacular things may move emotions, but the change is not permanent. Regeneration comes through faith, and faith comes through hearing the message of the gospel (see Romans 10:9–17). May I suggest that the tremendous success of the Pentecostal movement worldwide has little to do with their emphasis on miracles. Their success is due to the fact that no movement has taken the Great Commission in Matthew 28:18–20 more seriously, and no group has been more faithful in proclaiming the gospel. Take away that evangelistic and missionary thrust and I believe its growth would come to a sudden halt.

7

What are the best gifts?

Believers are commanded in 1 Corinthians 12:31 to "earnestly desire the higher gifts." The unavoidable implication is that some of the gifts are greater or better than others. The question is, which of the gifts are better, greater or "higher"? Another question is this: Since the Holy Spirit sovereignly bestows the gifts of the Spirit (Hebrews 2:4), why did the gifts disappear from the church after the first century according to some who hold to the cessationist position? I know that Pentecostal historians have attempted to trace the historical continuity of these gifts, but all have to admit they largely disappeared from church history, while many gifts remained.

Many fine studies have been done on spiritual gifts. I will not attempt to repeat them. However, I feel that frequently we miss the trees for the forest. Briefly, I would like to look at the gifts of the Holy Spirit, then ask a few questions and make some observations. I think it will help us to determine the *greater* gifts.

First, then, what makes a gift more desirable? We are not left in doubt as to the answer: it is that gift which strengthens or builds up, not just ourselves but the body of Christ. The KJV term is "edify." One of the more desirable gifts is prophecy, as it strengthens, encourages and comforts (1 Corinthians 14:3). We are warned against that which "puffs up" but does not build up (1 Corinthians 8:1). Selfishness must be avoided since we are part of the body, so gifts should be for the "common good" (1 Corinthians 12:7, NIV).

Having established this, let us examine the gifts of the Spirit. While I do not believe the lists in these passages are meant to be exhaustive, and other gifts may be filtered out by studying the epistles, I do think the lists in Figure 1 present an accurate, general picture of spiritual gifts. For comparative purposes, I list them in parallel columns. Two of the lists include offices. Gifts and offices should be understood as God giving gifts to men and giving gifted men to the church. Examine these lists closely.

We cannot positively identify what was involved in some gifts, such as the "word of wisdom" and the "word of knowledge." Faith may also be used differently from its more normal usage, i.e., it may refer to a special ministry, such as George Müller (1805–1898) and his orphanage work. But most gifts are easily identified, as they are referred to throughout the epistles.

Many have classified the gifts in different ways, but I would like to suggest the following very general classifications. First, there are *proclamation gifts*. These include prophecy, teaching, word of knowledge and tongues (when there is an interpreter). A second classification is *nurturing gifts*. This group covers service, exhortation (encouragement), giving, leading, showing mercy and helps. Discerning of spirits would probably be a nurturing gift, as it protects from false teachers.

A final classification is *sign gifts*. Here we find healing (as it seems to be a special gift, not just nurturing), working of miracles, tongues and interpretation of tongues. A sign is contrasted to a gradual healing or miracle, which cannot be observed by the human eye. The new birth is the greatest miracle of all, but is one that cannot be observed (John 3:8). Signs, on the other hand, serve as evidence (John 20:30–31). The gift of tongues is classified as a sign (1 Corinthians 14:22).

Figure 1. Key passages listing gifts of the Spirit

Romans 12:6–8	Ephesians 4:11	1 Corinthians 12:8–11	1 Corinthians 12:28–29
prophecy	apostles	word of wisdom	apostles
service	prophets	word of knowledge	prophets
teaching	evangelists	faith	teachers
exhortation	pastors	gifts of healing	miracles
giving	teachers	working of miracles	gifts of healing
leadership		prophecy	helping
mercy		discerning of spirits	administration
		tongues	tongues
		interpretation of tongues	interpretation of tongues

In examining these classifications in light of the teaching epistles, some observations can be made. First, the nurturing and proclamation gifts appear repeatedly and frequently in the epistles. While the particular phrases "the word of wisdom" and "word of knowledge" are not used, the need for wisdom and knowledge is a prominent New Testament theme. Next, it should be noted that the sign gifts are seldom mentioned. They are absent from the lists in Romans 12 and Ephesians 4. Apart from 1 Corinthians 12 and 14, they are only mentioned in Galatians 3:5 and Hebrews 2:4. James 5:14 does not seem to refer to a sudden healing or the use of a gift. The elders, not healers, are involved. It is also questionable whether the main emphasis of James 5:14 is physical rather than spiritual.

While the frequency of a particular teaching does not determine its importance, it does have significance. Over-emphasizing any doctrine of the New Testament, including baptism and communion, to the neglect of others, creates problems. Over-emphasizing a minor doctrine to the neglect of others is sure to create an even greater problem.

Another observation is in order. The sign gifts are more showy gifts. Many of the nurturing gifts are not showy, and can go unnoticed. *Does that mean they are the less important gifts, not to be eagerly desired?* Not at all! I think just the opposite is true. The greatest teacher is our Lord Jesus himself and he has something to say about the matter.

First of all, sign gifts in themselves do not impress the Lord. Matthew 7:22–23 tells us of people, who at the judgement will say, "Lord, Lord, did we not prophesy in your name, and cast out demons in your name, and do many mighty works in your name?" Our Lord will not be impressed, but will say, "I never knew you; depart from me, you workers of lawlessness." It is possible, then, to manifest some of the sign gifts without knowing the Lord and having a life characterized by obedience.

Another judgement scene involving our Lord is presented in Matthew 25:31–46. We will not look at the possible implications regarding the nation of Israel, but only at the principles presented. What impressed the King? It is those who helped the poor, the hungry, the sick, the stranger and the prisoner. There are no sign gifts referred to here. The sick are cared for, but not miraculously healed. Indeed, what is commended here are some of the lowest profile nurturing gifts: encouragement, giving, showing mercy and helping. In addition, those who were manifesting these gifts were not even aware of it, and I think that is particularly significant.

Evidently, the sign gifts are not necessarily evidence of knowing and obeying God. The non-showy gifts, which reach out to others, manifest the Spirit of Christ and are evidence of faith and obedience. James tells us the evidence of real faith is seen in our compassionate works for others (James 2:14–18). In addition, the sign gifts may be exercised without love (1 Corinthians 13:1–3), but not the nurturing gifts. Nurturing requires love and, in that way, is distinguished from mere welfare carried out by a hired social worker. As someone said, "You can give without loving, but you cannot love without giving."

A consideration of these facts should help us answer some important questions regarding the gifts of the Spirit and whether or not the Holy Spirit was inactive in the church from the second through nineteenth centuries. The best gifts are simply those that encourage, strengthen and build up. Prophecy is just one of them and is compared with tongues when it is declared a better gift.

Those gifts that build up, such as teaching, encouraging, giving, helping, showing mercy and serving are the gifts repeatedly emphasized in the teaching epistles. Furthermore, these are the gifts that have been present wherever true believers have been found in *every* period of church history. The idea that the Holy Spirit had to settle for lesser gifts for nineteen centuries is ludicrous. These are the gifts that impress the King and these are the gifts that the Holy Spirit has continually and universally used to build up the body of Christ. Therefore, these must be the *best* gifts.

Furthermore, these gifts may be manifested without the person even being aware they possess that gift. This is in keeping with Matthew 25:37–39. If this be the case, then we should redefine a "charismatic" church. Are not the *real* charismatic churches those which manifest these best gifts?

I am privileged to pastor a church that responds to needs in ways that continually amaze me. I have watched them give their time and substance to help others. When a need arises, I have no difficulty organizing people to respond. They will take turns sitting with someone in a hospital or driving someone to another city for medical treatment. When we had a baby with Down syndrome as part of our church family, we needed a special program of patterning to help him learn behaviour. Dozens from our church responded and gave their time to help the family through these long hours of patterning. It was featured in an article in a youth magazine published by *Back to the Bible* broadcast.[1]

The point I am trying to make is this: I believe I am pastoring a truly *charismatic* church, even though we do not emphasize the sign gifts. There are a number of churches in our city, which call themselves charismatic, but I believe none are more charismatic than our church in manifesting these *best* gifts. Most, if not all, of those in our church manifesting these gifts would not consider themselves charismatic.

The problem lies in the fact that, when we talk about spiritual gifts, these are not the ones that immediately come to mind. They

---

[1] Wendy MacDonnell, "Jeffrey," *Young Ambassadors* (October 1985): 50.

are not particularly exciting and therefore not usually sought after. If people were asked to form two lines to receive spiritual gifts, an interesting test could be made. One line would be for the gifts of teaching, giving, helping, showing mercy and serving. The other line would be for miracles, healings and tongues. Which line do you think would fill up first? No wonder Paul had to say, "earnestly desire the higher gifts" (1 Corinthians 12:31). This was simply another way of saying, "earnestly desire the higher gifts that will strengthen, encourage and comfort."

If one can accept this, they are well on their way to answering another question: *Why did the sign gifts disappear from common usage in the church for nineteen centuries?* Examining the problems encountered with the sign gifts in the early church and in the contemporary church does help uncover an answer.

It is my opinion that problems with these sign gifts caused them to be de-emphasized in the early church, without a conscious attempt to remove them from church life. The fact that problems arose, reinforces the conviction that they were not meant to be permanent, but only a temporary manifestation to authenticate a movement in redemptive history.

What are these problems? One problem is that they tend to be *self-centred*—that is especially true of tongues. Paul had to address the problem of people being blessed themselves, but not blessing others (1 Corinthians 14:1–25). If the gift is more of a blessing to you than to others, then that gift has a built-in, not a build-up, problem. I have had people tell me of visiting a Pentecostal church, and someone screamed out in tongues, frightening them. The person who screamed would probably respond by saying the visitor should have been "more open to the moving of the Spirit." However, since it was under their control (see 1 Corinthians 14:26–33), that person was showing a lack of sensitivity to the visitor. Therefore, the basic purpose of the gifts, edifying the body of Christ, has been violated. Even worse, to go into a non-charismatic church and manifest these gifts can cause actual division in the body of Christ. The gifts of the Spirit should unite and not divide the body (1 Corinthians 12:4–26). The nurturing gifts tend to unite the body, as by their nature they are other-centred rather than self-centred. The sign gifts have a tendency to become self-centred or at least call attention to self.

The second problem with sign gifts grows out of the first: they can lead to pride more readily than other gifts. They are showy and spectacular. The person manifesting them can be given the glory rather than God (Acts 14:6–15; 28:3–6). It was probably the manifestation of some of these sign gifts that caused Simon the Sorcerer to try to buy the power of the Holy Spirit (Acts 8:18–24). One who has the gift of miracles is far more susceptible to pride than someone with the gift of helping or showing mercy.

We are living in the days of the personality cult. It is by no means unique to Pentecostalism, but it is most prominent among those who claim the gift of healing or miracles. People will travel thousands of miles or kilometres just to be touched by that person. That which calls attention to self is also that which can lead to pride. Pride is destructive both to the individual and to the church (Proverbs 16:18; 1 Corinthians 8:1–11).

A third problem with the sign miracles is that they can be counterfeited. Of course, Satan's counterfeit of miracles goes back at least to Moses, when the Egyptian magicians used dark magic to create snakes out of their staffs (Exodus 7:11–12). In addition, sign gifts can be faked without supernatural means, and thus deceive a lot of people. A Marjoe Gortner can learn to speak in "tongues" and pass himself off as a faith healer.[2] It is much more difficult to fake nurturing gifts on a consistent basis, since they do not appeal to the unregenerate. Because the sign gifts can be self-serving, they do appeal to the unregenerate person.

First Corinthians 13 has sometimes been called a parenthesis between chapter 12 and 14, which deal with spiritual gifts. It is not parenthetical, but an essential part of understanding the proper use of the gifts. Some have suggested that Paul is promoting love, instead of the gifts as "a better way" (1 Corinthians 13:31). This is not the case.

Love and the gifts have a common function: *edification* (1 Corinthians 8:1; 14:12). This function is best achieved when they work together—in other words, spiritual gifts used in love. When the spiritual gifts are used selfishly or through pride, they are destructive rather than constructive. The reverse is also true: when the operation of spiritual gifts is destructive, they are not being

---

[2] See Chapter 5.

used with love. Charismatics need to ask themselves some tough questions: When the manifestation of certain gifts causes division among *true* believers, can it really be a work of the Holy Spirit in light of Galatians 5:22? Can you have the proper operation of the *gifts of the Spirit* without seeing the *fruit of the Spirit*? We know the Holy Spirit will rebuke sin, but when sincere Christians are torn apart over the gifts, something is radically wrong. 1 Corinthians 13 puts the responsibility on the one exercising the gifts.

It seems to me the reason sign gifts waned in the early church is both theological and pragmatic. Maybe the two go together? God never intended the sign gifts to be a continuing, normal part of church life because of the problems that arose. It is difficult to deny that Paul, while affirming their validity, was also throwing a wet blanket on their use in the church (1 Corinthians 14:39–40).

Having said all of this, I would like to also say a word in defence of the Pentecostals. Some of the most warm and loving people you can meet are Pentecostals. They would never consciously do anything to harm the body of Christ. They do manifest the gifts that I call the greater gifts. I personally am a debtor to more Pentecostal people than I can recall.

It is a case of practice being better than official doctrine. Because Pentecostal people experience the new birth, the Holy Spirit bestows these *best* gifts on Pentecostal people, just as he has upon believers of all ages. I have seen sincere Pentecostals desperately seeking the gift of tongues, when they were *already manifesting many of the nurturing gifts* in a most loving way. They already *had* the Holy Spirit but did not know it. I remember numerous occasions when, together with other Pentecostal ministers, we would express our consternation over someone who seemed so spiritual although they had not spoken in tongues, while others who had spoken in tongues seemed so carnal. It is not a puzzle anymore. The carnal ones probably did not have a genuine gift of tongues, but that was not the problem—they simply were not yielded to the Holy Spirit. The loving, spiritual ones were.

8

A second work?

At the time I left the Pentecostal ministry, I still believed in some kind of second work that constituted the baptism or infilling of the Holy Spirit. It would be a few more years before I changed my viewpoint. Strangely enough, it would come while observing a movement making the rounds in Baptist churches.

I was initially forced out of the Pentecostal ministry when I could no longer accept the belief that only those who had spoken in tongues were filled with the Holy Spirit. I still believed tongues might be *an* evidence, but not the *only* one, and I still believed in a special, second experience following regeneration.

Many groups believe in some kind of second experience. The Holiness groups call it "sanctification." Some of the more perfectionist groups refer to "eradication," meaning the "old man" or sinful nature is pulled out by its roots so only the "new man" remains: as a result, the person *cannot* sin. However, I have found most believe they *can* still make "mistakes." I had rejected that concept when I discovered God's passing grade for righteousness to be 100 per cent. In reality, "mistakes" *are* sins.

Other groups may refer to being baptized or filled with the Spirit, but without speaking in tongues. What I encountered about fifteen years ago in Baptist circles was the renewal movement. Speakers were holding meetings in churches to awaken apathetic members. The central emphasis was upon confession of sin and accepting the lordship of Christ in their lives. It is possible, they said, to be a Christian and receive Christ as Saviour, but not to have received him as Lord. To do this, one must confess all hidden sin in their lives and surrender completely to Christ as Lord. The people who did so would experience "renewal." At the close of the meetings, testimony services were encouraged, which they called "afterglow" meetings. Initially, I was very enthusiastic about the movement, but soon I observed the same problem I had experienced in Pentecostalism.

The early Pentecostal movement had direct links to the Holiness Movement, which originated out of early Methodism. They believed in a *second* work of grace called sanctification. The Pentecostals added a *third* work called the baptism of the Holy Spirit, and so had three works of grace. There was considerable tension in those early days between those who held to the three works of grace and those who believed in the finished work of the cross. Some modern Pentecostal denominations can trace their roots to a division over that doctrine.

My father strongly held to the finished work of the cross, so I naturally followed suit. At the same time, I believed in a second work or baptism of the Holy Spirit, although I would not refer to it as a second work of grace. It seemed evident to me that people did have a second experience and usually spoke in tongues. The scriptural evidence for this was in the Book of Acts. At Samaria, people repented and were baptized, but had not evidenced the Holy Spirit (Acts 8:15–16). Paul was converted on the road to Damascus, but later filled with the Holy Spirit (Acts 9:17). The ultimate proof came at Ephesus where Paul asked, "Did you receive the Holy Spirit when you believed?" (Acts 19:2) Those verses were sufficient to prove to me that being filled with the Holy Spirit was an experience *subsequent* to saving faith.

I began to question this two-tier Christianity when I became disillusioned with the charismatic movement in 1963. It was pointed out to me that 1 Corinthians 12:13 says, "For in one Spirit we were all baptized into one body" Here, the baptism of the Holy Spirit is equated with initial regeneration and new birth by the Holy Spirit (see also John 3:5–8). If the baptism of the Holy Spirit makes us part of the body of Christ, how can it be *subsequent* to salvation?

The explanation Pentecostals give is there are *two* baptisms. One is *by* the Holy Spirit placing us into the body of Christ. The second—promised by John the Baptist—is done by Jesus, who will "baptize you *with* the Holy Spirit and fire" (Matthew 3:11). There is a difference we are told, between being baptized *by* the Holy Spirit and *with* the Holy Spirit. That answer satisfied me for a while. However, as I studied New Testament Greek, I discovered it was the same preposition in both passages and it could be translated as *by, in* or *with*. For a Greek person to understand this as *two* baptisms of the Holy Spirit in the New Testament texts, he would have to be sharp on syntax. I was troubled by this enough that I changed my terminology. I felt the experience subsequent to conversion should be referred to as the *infilling* of the Spirit, rather than the *baptism* of the Spirit. Nevertheless, I still held there was a *second* work.

The problem one encounters with any form of second work is the creation of *two distinct levels of Christianity*. It divided those who had this experience from those who did not. It especially hit me in 1973, while I was pastoring a Baptist church in Moncton, New Brunswick. Some of our people were going to retreats where confession of sin and surrendering to the lordship of Christ was being emphasized. A number were "renewed" and came back to our church on spiritual fire. They shared their testimonies and urged the rest to get out of the doldrums of Christianity and find renewal. I was excited because I thought we were in for a revival. I had heard reports of revival sweeping churches throughout the renewal movement.

Two things happened that dampened my enthusiasm. First, the fire quickly died out in most of them. It did not make them more faithful in church attendance, more diligent in church work or better witnesses of the gospel. They mainly wanted their "afterglow" or sharing meetings. I became alarmed as I felt some of the testimonies bordered on exhibitionism.

The second problem was even more serious. I quickly sensed a spirit of superiority in those who had been renewed. They felt they were a notch better than the ones who were still "carnal" and tended to look down on the unrenewed. If you had not been renewed, you just were not with it. Years later, one woman in another church told me she could not find good fellowship in our church because the people were not on her spiritual wavelength. I displayed my lack of renewal, by telling her she was full of spiritual pride.

It was this same air of spiritual superiority I had found repulsive while a Pentecostal. Those who had the "baptism" looked down on those who did not. Other denominations who do not have the charismatic experience are looked upon as second-class citizens. It might be difficult to get them to admit it, but there is a spirit of proselytism among Pentecostals as they believe other Christians need to come up to their level. All those who promote a second work of the Holy Spirit tend to develop this type of thinking.

While I still believed people needed a second work, I was increasingly disturbed by a mentality that made one Christian feel he was superior to his fellow believer. I once heard Dr. Alan Redpath preach at Moody Memorial Church in Chicago that the "Bible doesn't teach sinless perfection; it teaches sinful corruption" and "the only good thing about the Christian is Jesus." That struck a responsive chord. Were not all Christians sinners saved *by grace*? Did we not all stand equal at the foot of the cross? After we had done our best, we were still only unprofitable or "unworthy servants" (Luke 17:10).

When I saw this happening, I put the damper on the renewal movement in our Baptist church. I did not carry through with plans to have one of the renewal leaders come for special services. This meant our church avoided any serious division over renewal. Other churches who had renewal meetings seemed to inevitably experience sharp division within a year. To be fair, I am prepared to admit the renewal movement has helped many. People do need to confess sin in their lives and surrender to the lordship of Christ (James 5:16). However, it should not be made into a second experience to be shared in public, but a daily experience between themselves and their Lord. As well, no doctrine, however biblical, should be overemphasized. An overemphasis on confession of sin can lead to an unhealthy introspection.

Something else came out of my observation of the renewal movement. Many who thought they had been *renewed* had really been *made new*. What they actually experienced was the new birth! They had been church members by profession, but had failed to fully commit their lives to Christ. When confronted with the lordship of Christ, they now made that commitment.

Seeing this made me wonder just how many church members have never really passed from death unto life. I began to seriously question whether one could receive Christ as Saviour and then still live a carnal Christian life until, sometime down the road, you decided to receive Christ as Lord. Could we come to Christ and say, "I will accept your benefits, but not your dominion." As I studied the Gospels, I could not find a two-tier discipleship. Following Christ seemed to be *all or nothing* (Luke 14:24–33). If that was the case, where does it leave a second work?

It was not until a few years later, in 1975, that my thinking culminated in rejecting a second work. During that summer, we decided to combine business and pleasure on a trip to the West Coast. My wife and one-year-old son accompanied me while I attended summer school at Regent College, Vancouver, British Columbia. One course I took was on the book of Colossians and it was taught by Dr. J.I. Packer (1926–2020). The heresy in Colossians was what he called a "gospel of extras." The focal point is Colossians 2:9–10,

> For in him the whole fullness of deity dwells bodily, and you have been filled [*lit.* "made full"] in him, who is the head of all rule and authority.

The point is: you cannot *add* to fullness. If you try, you will inevitably take away. In Christ, we *have* fullness and therefore, we need nothing more. When we initially receive Christ, we receive fullness, and so the need for a second work of the Holy Spirit is eliminated. We simply need to walk in the fullness we have received, "Therefore, as you received Christ Jesus the Lord, so walk in him" (Colossians 2:6).

The error of the Christians at Colossae was to add astrology and other religious practices to their basic trust in Christ. Of course, faith must have the other side of the coin, repentance (Acts 20:21), but not as a *separate* work. Repentance is not simply a change of mind as the New Testament Greek word can mean, but also has the Old Testament meaning of a radical reorientation of the entire life. To repent in the Old Testament meant "to return." Idols were destroyed, altars rebuilt and obedience to the Law resumed. New Testament discipleship has these same radical demands. When you come to Christ, you come to one who is *both* Saviour and Lord (Romans 10:9–10).

Now, it must be admitted that many people have a crisis experience after they are saved when they realize the full implications of the lordship of Christ. However, this is not a second work, but an outgrowth of the initial work of the Holy Spirit. Justification cannot be separated from sanctification. We are not declared holy so we can remain unholy in practice. We are declared holy so we become holy. While we are saved from the *penalty* of sin in a moment, we are saved from the *power* of sin progressively throughout our life. Allowing that one may experience a second, third or fourth crisis, the Christian life is basically a walk, not a pogo stick journey.

Growing in holiness is growing in our sense of unworthiness. If Paul considered himself the foremost of sinners (1 Timothy 1:15), can we consider ourselves less? Any experience that makes us feel superior to our brother or sister does us a disservice. Someone has said, "There are only two classes of people, sinners who believe they are righteous, and the righteous who know they are sinners." Or as another put it, "Witnessing is one beggar telling another beggar where to find bread."

Christians may differ from others so strongly that they form different fellowships. These differences may be over baptism, eschatology or church order. At the same time, they should not feel they are superior to the others, in the sense of having more of Christ than others do. It is difficult to avoid a superior feeling when you believe you have more truth. It is almost impossible to keep from feeling superior if you think you have had a greater experience. That is the error of the "second work" proponents.

I do not intend to belittle experiences. We should remember

and thank the Lord for our spiritual experiences, but we need to keep them in perspective. In the ultimate analysis, we are saved by pure grace. The Puritan Thomas Watson had the right perspective when he prayed, "Our prayers need pardon, and our tears need the blood sprinkling to wash them."[1] It is possible to be proud of our repentance.

If one rejects a "second work," how can the time lapse between believing and receiving the Holy Spirit be explained in the Book of Acts? First of all, one should go back to John 20:22 and note that Jesus gave the Holy Spirit in a pre-ascension encounter. We read, "And when he had said this, he breathed on them and said to them, 'Receive the Holy Spirit.'" Here Jesus, at least symbolically, gave the Holy Spirit to the entire church. Acts records four initial outpourings of the Holy Spirit on different groups of people: the Jews in Acts 2, the Samaritans in Acts 8, Cornelius and the Gentiles in Acts 10 and the disciples of John the Baptist in Acts 19. In each case, some external manifestation confirmed this giving of the Holy Spirit. Also, in each case, apostolic authority was involved, twice by the laying on of hands. These cases were obviously special, as the church became universal. Acts 19:2 should be translated, "Did you receive the Holy Spirit *when* you believed?" (emphasis added) rather than "*since* you believed," as some translations render it. It is literally, "upon believing" or "having believed." The obvious implication is that people were expected to have received the Holy Spirit at the time of believing. That was the normal pattern, and is in harmony with Galatians 3:2, "Let me ask you only this: Did you receive the Spirit by works of the law or by hearing with faith?" The delay between Saul's encounter with Christ on the road to Damascus and receiving the Holy Spirit through the ministry of Ananias is in keeping with the New Testament pattern of human agency always being present in evangelism (eg. the angel directing Cornelius to Peter and the Holy Spirit sending Philip to the Ethiopian eunuch).

The question that naturally follows is: What does it mean to be "filled with the Spirit"? The clearest passage is Ephesians 5:18, "And do not get drunk with wine, for that is debauchery, but be

---

[1] Iain H. Murray, ed., *Sermons of the Great Ejection* (London: Banner of Truth, 1962), 115.

filled with the Spirit." Many have pointed out that *filled* does not refer to a single act in the original language. This is correct, as the Greek is a present passive imperative, meaning, "Be continually being filled." The Williams translation puts it, "Be ever filled." The same people could be filled with the Spirit on more than one occasion (Acts 2:4; 4:8; 4:31). It is not because, as we used to say when I was a Pentecostal "some leak," but because the fullness of the Spirit is a life rather than a single act. Remember, the Spirit is not a *thing* or *force*, but a *Person*.[2] It is clear when you examine Ephesians 5:14–21 that Paul is discussing "being filled with the Spirit" as a lifestyle and not a single event. As someone has said, "We don't get more of the Spirit, but the Spirit has more of us."

Understanding it to be a lifestyle, and looking closely at Paul's words, helps us to identify the meaning of being "filled with the Spirit." The "and" in verse 18 connects it with verse 17, which states, "Therefore do not be foolish, but understand what the will of the Lord is." Also, note that being filled with the Spirit is contrasted with being drunk with wine. It does not mean that being filled with the Spirit makes us *act* like we are drunk, as some Pentecostals suggest. The context tells us to always be in full control of our faculties. The noise on the Day of Pentecost made some think the believers were drunk, but it was denied by Peter (Acts 2:15). The point of verse 18 is that, instead of being *controlled* by wine, we are to be controlled by the Holy Spirit. In other words, we have a life controlled by the Holy Spirit, obeying or responding to the will of God as referred to in verse 17.

When we grasp this, we understand being filled with the Spirit is primarily a matter of *obedience* rather than *experience*. This is an important concept and constitutes a major theme of the New Testament. A stable Christian life is simply a matter of knowing and doing the will of God. The similarity between Ephesians and Colossians is evident, and noted by most commentators. Paul probably wrote them a short time apart. Similar to comparing the

---

[2] The United Pentecostal Church (UPC) believes the Holy Spirit is the *essence* of God the Father, not a separate *person*, in the same way each human has a spirit. The problem with this is the UPC are trying to make God in human being's image, rather than human being's in God's image. This false belief about the Holy Spirit may have led to the confusion of the "filling of the Spirit" as an *essence* that can "leak," rather than a *Person* who indwells and permanently seals the believers (Ephesians 1:13–14).

synoptic Gospels, it is good to compare Ephesians and Colossians. Corresponding to Ephesians 5:18–19 is Colossians 3:16. There is a connection between being "filled with the Spirit" and "Let the word of Christ dwell in you richly." A life controlled by God's Word and will is a life filled with the Spirit. The evidence of this life is seen in how we build up others through worship, teaching and fellowship.

I have been a bit turned off by books promoting some "secret" of the victorious Christian life. It is not a secret. Rather, it is clear and simple: Know and do God's will! As Paul states in Romans 12:1–2:

> I appeal to you therefore, brothers, by the mercies of God, to present your bodies as a living sacrifice, holy and acceptable to God, which is your spiritual worship. Do not be conformed to this world, but be transformed by the renewal of your mind, that by testing you may discern what is the will of God, what is good and acceptable and perfect.

It should be pointed out, while it may be *simple*, it is anything but *easy*.

In the Sermon on the Mount, Jesus taught the importance of knowing and doing the will of God (Matthew 7:21–27). In verses 21–23, we see that a fantastic experience is not enough. Even prophecy, exorcism and miracles can result in zero, when it comes to God's commendation. In verses 24–27, we discover that the stable Christian life—capable of surviving the storms of life—is founded upon hearing and doing Christ's words. Jesus carefully shows that the key to a stable Christian life is not *experience* (v. 22), but *obedience* (v. 24).

As Protestants, we affirm the principle of *sola Scriptura*—by Scripture alone. A believer's authority is not found in tradition or ecclesiastical office, but in the Bible. We must also reject experience as an authority, and judge all things by Scripture. Of course, as Matthew 7:26 points out, the Bible must be heeded and not just heard.

A final word needs to be said about the *unique* authority of Scripture. *Can we have an authoritative word from God today?* To answer that question we must ask: Do we have apostles and prophets today? Prophets were spokespersons who proclaimed a direct word from God: thus, the frequent use of, "and the Word of the LORD came unto me" in the prophetic books of the Old Testament.

In the New Testament, the apostles were a special group with special authority, as eyewitnesses of the resurrection. Whether Paul was meant to take the place of Judas instead of Matthias, is not important. Paul was definitely called by God as a special apostle (1 Corinthians 15:8–9). The term *apostle* is occasionally used in the New Testament for someone who is sent (2 Corinthians 8:23)[3] and is the equivalent of a missionary (*apostle* is derived from the Greek and *missionary* from the Latin), but "the apostles" was a special designation for those with a special commission. They spoke with divine authority and could confer the Holy Spirit by the laying on of hands.

The duration of the apostolic and prophetic offices is established in Ephesians 2:20 where they are said to be foundational. By its very nature, a foundation is non-repeatable and serves as a standard for the rest of the structure. While the apostolic office no longer exists, the apostolic *ministry* (and therefore apostolic succession) continues in that ministry, which is faithful to the apostolic foundation and witness. The New Testament, of course, comprises the apostolic witness given to the church.

Likewise, the prophetic office no longer exists, but the prophetic *ministry* continues in the church, with the proclamation of the Word of God. The Holy Spirit is given to *all* Christians to exercise a ministry of proclamation (Acts 2:17), although some may have a special gift of proclaiming the Word of God. The content of proclamation today is the "and we have the prophetic word more fully confirmed" (2 Peter 1:19), which is further identified as the "prophecy of Scripture" (2 Peter 1:20). Therefore, prophetic ministry today is the proclamation of God's Word as found in the Bible. The mysteries and knowledge God would have us know (1 Corinthians 13:2) are contained in the completed canon of the Bible.

While recognizing that we are open to the charge of having a "paper pope" and a religion that is only intellectual, we must

---

[3] The term *messengers* (KJV, ESV) is literally *apostles* (NASB) in 2 Corinthians 8:23.

remain "people of the Book." If 2 Timothy 3:16–17[4] is true, then the Bible is *sufficient* to lead us into a mature Christian life. A *second* work or special experience is unnecessary. We should heed the words of 2 Timothy 2:15, "Do your best to present yourself to God as one approved, a worker who has no need to be ashamed, rightly handling the word of truth," and of James 1:22, "But be doers of the word, and not hearers only, deceiving yourselves."

---

[4] "All Scripture is breathed out by God and profitable for teaching, for reproof, for correction, and for training in righteousness, that the man of God may be complete, equipped for every good work."

9

Problems in the upper room

When I left Pentcostalism in 1971, Pentecostals and charismatics had problems, and those problems have not disappeared. In fact, some have escalated. In spite of attempts to give the appearance that charismatics can cope with anything, all is not well in the upper room.

I hope this will not be seen as an attack on those I consider my brothers and sisters in Christ. I have sometimes thought I should go back to the Pentecostal church and apologize for saying that Pentecostals had all the crackpots. It seems there are plenty of crackpots to go around. Baptists have lots of them too. I guess we should remember the words of A.W. Tozer (1897–1963) who said, "God uses all kinds of vessels, including those that are a bit cracked." The fellow I see wearing the "Repent or perish" T-shirt is my brother.

I also used to think the problem of clergy being involved in immorality was more common among Pentecostals than anywhere else. However, Baptists have their fair share of that too. It is wrong to suggest, because of media attention, that Pentecostals are emotionally unstable or morally loose as a whole. In my opinion, some of God's choicest saints are in Pentecostal churches.

Nevertheless, there are some serious problems inherent to the Pentecostal movement. One that has already been alluded to is emotionalism. Now, emotion is important; the issue is not intellect *versus* emotion. For change to be effective in this life, it must involve *both* the mind and the heart. For example, sorrow *in itself* is not repentance, but it can lead to repentance (2 Corinthians 7:10).

The problem arises when emotion is emphasized to the point that people go to church looking primarily for an emotional feeling. If they go away feeling better, the service was a success. If not, the service was a failure. This puts pressure on the preacher to become a *performer*, and people are left vulnerable to be taken in by those like Marjoe Gortner.[1] A good performer, who can provide the emotional high people are seeking, can be well paid for his effort, and this helps to keep the fakes in business. If he is a good performer, people will frequently overlook moral and spiritual failure in his life. Even today, there are known adulterers who have had multiple divorces and yet carry on successful charismatic ministries.

I have yet to meet a Bible expositor who was a fake, in the sense he had never believed in God or the Bible. Many may fail but few, if any, are phonies. When the expectation of the church is for good biblical exposition week by week, phonies are not attracted. However, when the church wants a performer and will pay well for it, it invites charlatans. I am not suggesting expositors are non-existent among Pentecostals, or that fakes cannot be found among non-Pentecostals, but this problem is more prevalent in circles where emotional feeling is given top priority.

Closely related to emotionalism is that of *subjectivism*. When people claim God spoke to them or when they give a prophecy, it is natural for people to accept it as being from God. If the message begins, "Hear you my people" and ends with "and this is the Word of the Lord," does it have the same divine authority as Scripture? People have been told to sell their homes, quit their

---

[1] See Chapter 5.

jobs and even marry a certain person in the name of prophecy. Are we at the mercy of anyone who says God told them to tell us to do a certain thing? It is happening all the time in Pentecostal circles. People are told to send money because God spoke to this person telling them to instruct people to send money. The answer usually given is we must test it by Scripture (1 Thessalonians 5:20–22). However, not every possible situation is addressed in the Bible, like giving money for every type of appeal.

It is not an easy issue to resolve as we do not want to deny that God can verbally communicate with people today. I have never had God give me a direct message. I have had a strong sense that God was saying something to me, but never a word-by-word message. Nevertheless, I do not deny that possibility.

I think the best resolution is two-fold. First, the prophetic Word that God has for us to communicate to others today is *Scripture*. In other words, the only message from God for others must come from Scripture and be in harmony with proper methods of hermeneutics.[2] Second, God may communicate personally with us some messages regarding marriage, career, geographical residence or just about anything. It is usually not in an audible voice, but I am not excluding that possibility. The leading of the Lord is a whole subject in itself. However, this is something for us *personally*, and not for others. We may *advise* others on what we think about their career, marriage, decisions or whatever, but we can only *command* others when there is a command in Scripture on that matter. In the same vein, God may impress upon you to give money to a certain person or ministry, but God does not tell that person to demand it from you.

Therefore, I have rejected messages from people who told me God gave them a word for me. Recently, a young man came into my office. He had left our church years ago before I became pastor. He told me God had instructed him to come see me; I was to bring the "moving of the Spirit" and "miracles" to our church. While talking, he told me of the charismatic church he attended, and was critical of other charismatic churches. Knowing there are not good feelings among most of the charismatic churches in this city toward one another, I suggested he go out and get all

---

[2] Meaning, biblical interpretation.

of them to love one another, since the fruit of the Spirit is love. Following that, he could come back and straighten out us Baptists! (I am afraid the fruit of the Spirit may not have been over abundant in my own life at that particular time.)

Along with the emphasis on blessing and feeling has come a "gospel of prosperity." The Pentecostals are not the only ones preaching it, but they are at the forefront. "God not only wants you healthy, but he wants you wealthy," it is said. Of course, this is a very attractive message and lavish lifestyles of ministers have been justified by this teaching. But this view is totally incompatible with such passages such as 1 Timothy 6:6–10,

> But godliness with contentment is great gain, for we brought nothing into the world, and we cannot take anything out of the world. But if we have food and clothing, with these we will be content. But those who desire to be rich fall into temptation, into a snare, into many senseless and harmful desires that plunge people into ruin and destruction. For the love of money is a root of all kinds of evils. It is through this craving that some have wandered away from the faith and pierced themselves with many pangs.

I am all for the clergy having an adequate and even comfortable living, and am not adverse to quoting 1 Timothy 5:17–18,

> Let the elders who rule well be considered worthy of double honor, especially those who labor in preaching and teaching. For the Scripture says, "You shall not muzzle an ox when it treads out the grain," and, "The laborer deserves his wages."

I also know Christians with whom God has entrusted considerable wealth and they have been good stewards. I have yet to meet a preacher who could handle wealth, but I am sure some exist. We should be prepared, as Paul, to accept bounty or lack as both come from the Lord (Philippians 4:11–12). *Contentment* with God's dealings with us is key for the Christian in regards to both health and wealth.

What is most disturbing about this gospel of prosperity is the suggestion that health and wealth are *evidence* of God's love and blessing. It is repeating the error of Job's friends who judged character by suffering. A man's character should never be judged by his suffering. If anything, a man's suffering should be judged by his character.

At the root of the error is seeing physical or material prosperity to be evidence of God's love. The Bible is very clear. There is *one* incontrovertible proof of God's love—and that is *the cross* (Romans 5:6–8). The Christian should never ask for additional proof. Our worth to God is seen at Calvary. Proper self-esteem looks to the cross and not at a financial balance sheet or medical record.

It is not wrong to desire physical wealth (3 John 2). Nor is it wrong to desire a comfortable lifestyle for our family. I also think it is proper to pray for these things, but doing so while asking for God's will to be done. In fact, we should ask for God's will before we even ask for our essential needs as seen in the Lord's Prayer (Matthew 6:10–11). The modern "name it and claim it" movement is especially disturbing when they demand health and wealth from God. Our value system should be based on *spiritual* health and wealth. Our priority is the kingdom of God and his righteousness (Matthew 6:33). We should never judge a person's spiritual condition by sickness or poverty. Some of the greatest stories of Christian witness and discipleship are coming out of Third World countries where nothing is known of our "gospel of prosperity."[3]

The media have begun to focus on the personal lifestyles of the religious leaders in North America. They are posing a question churches should be asking themselves: How can they justify living in multi-million-dollar homes when they are followers of the One who said, "Foxes have holes, and birds of the air have nests, but the Son of Man has nowhere to lay his head" (Matthew 8:20)? That is a valid question which must be answered. Pentecostals should be concerned about this as the chief offenders are those who claim to be filled with the Spirit and to possess a superior brand of Christianity.

Another serious issue for Pentecostals is the whole area of physical healing. The pastor I served with in Indiana was brought

---

[3] Since the time of writing, regrettably the "health and wealth gospel" has become pervasive in much of the Third World.

up in a church which taught that it was sinful to go to doctors or dentists or to take any medicine. One should trust God, and if they had faith, God would perform the operation, fill teeth or even strengthen eyes so eyeglasses were not needed. This pastor had somewhat modified his views and his wife would occasionally ask me for a "faith aid," meaning an aspirin. I used to keep a package with me in case of a headache.

Most Pentecostals have moderated their views on healing to the point that they readily accept medical help. In fact, the leading faith healer of our time has built a hospital and medical school.[4] Many Pentecostals now pray for healing "if it be thy will." That puts them squarely in the camp of Baptists and others who will pray for the recovery of those who are sick if it is God's will and by whatever means he chooses.

More germane to the subject is the question of physical healing in the atonement. The passages appealed to are Isaiah 53:4–5 and its quotation in Matthew 8:17, which says, "He took our illnesses and bore our diseases." That sickness is one of the results of the fall of humanity, we can readily admit. It is also true that as a result of the cross, all effects of sin will ultimately be removed from our lives. This includes physical suffering (Revelation 21:4).

The problem arises when you put deliverance from sickness *on the same level* as deliverance from sin as a benefit of the atonement. There is forgiveness of sin and eternal life for all who ask (John 3:16; Acts 2:21; Revelation 22:17)—that is guaranteed by the atonement. Therefore, everyone living in sin is out of God's will. Is the same thing true about sickness? What about death, is it also never God's will? There are some real problems seeing physical healing guaranteed by the atonement. It would mean everyone desiring physical healing should find it, as everyone desiring forgiveness of sin can find it.

The fact is, Isaiah 53 is concerned about God visiting his people through the suffering Servant. He would identify with their suffering and sorrows. Matthew 8:17 is properly quoting Isaiah 53:4 and identifying Christ with God's visitation. He shared with their sufferings and sorrows, thus the physical healings identify him with Isaiah 53. Actually, the issues being dealt

---

[4] Phil was most likely referring to Oral Roberts (1918–2009) who built a hospital and medical school in the 1980s.

with in Isaiah 53 were primarily spiritual. Verse 5 refers to "transgressions," "iniquities" and "peace" (or "well being"). Therefore, it is natural to understand "healed" as continuing the primarily spiritual theme. The apostle Peter quotes Isaiah 53:5 and applies it in a spiritual sense, "He himself bore our sins in his body on the tree, that we might die to sin and live to righteousness. By his wounds you have been healed" (1 Peter 2:24).

It is true that Christ still cares about our hurts and sorrows of whatever nature. We can go to him with our burdens and be assured he cares for us (1 Peter 5:7). It may be God *will* grant us physical healing. But on the other hand, he may choose to leave it with us to accomplish one of his purposes. In that case, he will provide grace to bear it. Healing is always available, but it may not include the physical. Christ died on the cross so that a young, resentful quadriplegic, full of bitterness, by the name of Joni Eareckson Tada, could find healing for her spirit.[5] If a lack of physical healing is proof of failure, then the apostle Paul failed when he left Trophimus ill at Miletus (2 Timothy 4:20).

The idea that enough faith will get you what you want is not warranted by Scripture. Since we are kept by the power of God through faith (1 Peter 1:5), we know God will take us through life by faith. However, the heroes of faith in Hebrews 11 sometimes had miraculous *deliverance* from trial and other times equally miraculous *endurance* in trial.

This raises the subject of miracles—another Pentecostal problem. Pentecostals will advertise "miracle services" or "miracles nights." It is important we believe God is a God of miracles. I believe it is even important to believe God can do something today that defies known phenomena. In most cases we do not experience it, but a healthy faith in God allows for it. My pastor for several years shared with my father about a visit from what he was sure was an angel, during a very difficult time in his life. This man, now with the Lord, was one of the sanest and most godly men I have ever met.[6] I would have believed it if he had said he

---

[5] You can read Joni's remarkable story in Joni Eareckson Tada, *Joni: An Unforgettable Story*, 45th anniversary ed. (Grand Rapids: Zondervan, 2021).
[6] The pastor referred to was Brother Earl Jacques who was Phil's pastor when he lived in Fredericton, New Brunswick, and attended the Fredericton United Pentecostal Church.

met little green Martians. He did not publicly talk about it and only shared it with my father because they were very close friends. This type of thing may happen, but I am convinced it is very rare.

However, I am also convinced we can see miracles in our lives that work through what is generally referred to as natural laws. What the world would attribute to chance or coincidence, the Christian may see as a miracle from God. Is that not what Hebrews 11:1 refers to as the product of faith? We see things that cannot be otherwise seen *through the eyes of faith*. Bible scholar F.F. Bruce explains, "Physical eyesight produces conviction or evidence of visible things; faith is the organ, which enables people…to see the invisible order."[7]

Faith is not superstition. Superstition is believing in things that *do not* exist. Faith "sees" things that *do* exist, only they cannot be seen with physical eyes. It is one of the great paradoxes—faith sees that which cannot be seen.

During my summer break in 1964, I desperately needed a high paying job so I could afford to finish my last term at college. It seemed a door was opening at one of the steel mills in East Chicago, Indiana. A foreman for one of the mills was a member of the church in Hammond, and assured me of a job. I applied and did not get it. There were too many workers who had sons who wanted summer jobs. They received priority treatment, so I looked elsewhere.

At the Veterans Administration (VA) office, the woman who interviewed me asked me if I could paint, to which I answered in the affirmative. In turn, she asked me if I could repair electrical fixtures, plumbing fixtures, floor tile, roofing shingles and a number of other things. Each time I answered, "Yes." So, she gave me a contract and I filled it in. She even helped me with pricing. When we left the office, the pastor turned to me and said, "Phil, I never realized you had done all of those things." I replied, "She didn't ask me that. She only asked me if I *could* do those things."

In short, I got the contract on the first house. It went well, so the nice woman at the VA office gave me all the contracts I could handle for the summer. By being the general contractor and doing the work myself, I avoided the middleman and reached a

---

[7] F.F. Bruce, *The Epistle to the Hebrews* (Grand Rapids: Eerdmans, 1964), 279.

height of affluence that summer I have not attained since. I finished college out of debt, a car paid for and money in my pocket. I considered it a miracle.

One day after college resumed, I was having coffee in the student center with my biology professor. I do not know his religious background, but he was a very warm and friendly fellow. He inquired about my summer. I related what had happened and finished by saying, "I really thank God for helping me out." He looked at me, smiled condescendingly, and said, "I find that God helps those who help themselves." I saw divine provision; he saw a young fellow who happened to get a lucky break and made the most of it.

I believe it is proper to think God is interested in every area of our life. Faith expects to see God work in answer to prayer. Faith rejoices when something special happens and gives the glory to God, but faith does not presume that God will always work things out in the way we desire. Sometimes God is working out purposes we cannot see and do not understand. Nevertheless, we should always believe God is active in our lives.

The danger in the Pentecostal movement is not the belief in the miraculous. The danger lies in the affinity for the dramatic and the sensational. Miracles, in the sense of God doing in our lives what would not normally take place, can be a regular occurrence; the dramatic and sensational are not. If we are hearing many sensational testimonies, we may become dissatisfied with what seems dull and routine in our own lives.

A final concern regarding the Pentecostal movement is the growing ecumenism. The charismatic movement has made some strange bedfellows. As a boy, I used to hear preachers denounce the ecumenical movement as being of the devil and the Roman Catholic Church as the "great whore of Babylon." Now, an Assemblies of God minister, a Roman Catholic priest and an executive from the World Council of Churches may share the same platform.

Let me say clearly that I am not an extreme separatist. I happen to now believe (and it did not come easily), that there are born-again Christians in both Roman Catholic churches and churches affiliated with the World Council of Churches. They are brothers and sisters, and I am prepared to accept them as such. I have learned the difference between acceptance and approval. I may accept someone as my brother in Christ while not approving of all he believes or does.

Furthermore, I endorse interdenominational efforts where Christians who differ over non-essential points of doctrine combine in a missionary or evangelistic enterprise. One of the great blessings of my life has been attending interdenominational schools where I met, fellowshipped and worked with other Christians who differed with me on many doctrinal issues. I have always tried to be a Christian first, and a Pentecostal or Baptist second.

Having said that, I would express my concern when people come together with the *only* common denominator being a belief in speaking in tongues. The charismatic movement now includes those who deny the verbal inspiration and inerrancy of Scripture. It also includes those who do not believe that salvation is by grace alone through faith. In fact, the charismatic movement has invaded just about every realm of Christianity.

I first recognized the dangers of the charismatic movement regarding ecumenism when I was still a Pentecostal pastor. In 1969, I came across a book by Marcus Bach recording his own experience with speaking in tongues.[8] I was greatly disturbed by it and had my father read it. He was perplexed too and had no explanation.

The first two chapters describe his experience in receiving the "baptism" of the Holy Spirit and speaking in tongues in a Pentecostal church in Milwaukee, Wisconsin. No Pentecostal could read it without being moved and convinced that he had the real thing. It was the typical story of someone from a staid, formal church coming in contact with Pentecostalism and finally receiving the "baptism." I read it and identified with it.

However, the book continued with his story of going on to university and beginning to study, not only Pentecostalism, but various other religious experiences. He even studied the drug scene, concluding it was equally valued with Christianity. I was shocked when I read about his visit with voodoo worshippers in Haiti. He wrote:

---

[8] Marcus Bach, *The Inner Ecstasy: The Power and Glory of Speaking in Tongues* (New York: World Publishing, 1969).

Deep within the collective mind that linked me with the total family of the children of God was ecstasy, the common ground of faith, and whether one found it on the sophisticated level of his culture in front of altars and statues or another discovered it in a printery, and still another on the damp floor of God's good earth, it was all the same. It was a universal encounter and who was to say who had experienced the highest joy? Ecstasy was a universal link in the chain of spiritual understanding. There was no question about it, these voodoo dervishes would go to their homes in the hills and jungles of their enchanted land, sink to their weathered tarps spread on the barren ground, and somewhere in the shadows they would catch vision of the elusive loa and of themselves as once, not many years ago, I too, had caught the shadow of the Holy Spirit the day I spoke in tongues.[9]

Perhaps Bach represents the extreme in making tongues the unifying force, but it does point to the problem. Someone can have an experience and be so taken up with it that nothing else matters. The issue is no longer *truth*, but *ecstasy*. The exclusiveness of Christianity is surrendered. If this happens, how can one take seriously the words of Christ, "I am the way, and the truth, and the life. No one comes to the Father except through me" (John 14:6)? Christ is not *a* way, but *the only* way.

I confess that I am a conservative fundamentalist[10] (just slightly left of the Flat Earth Society), but I have always tried to be open toward others who disagree with me. However, I cannot accept that which denies the exclusive claims of Christ. Our very existence is at stake. Experience must be tested by truth and not the other way around.

My concern lies in the fact that the charismatic movement has broken down some barriers that should have remained up. Syncretism is the enemy of Christianity and not its friend. The basic truths of the gospel are not open for negotiation.

---

[9] Bach, *Inner Ecstasy*, 116.
[10] Phil defined his fundamentalism as being committed to the fundamentals of the faith rather than radical separation that many fundamentalists are focused on. He put the "fun" in fundamentalism, as he majored in the Bible.

I find it disturbing to turn on my television and see a prominent clergyman approving homosexual marriages in an interview. Then I switch channels and see another clergyman of the same denomination on a religious talk show promoting speaking in tongues. How can a Spirit-filled man remain in that denomination? Is there no longer any ground for separation from sin and unbelief?

When I approach my Pentecostal friends regarding these issues, I am told I should not condemn, but just love and pray for them. There has been a dramatic change in the thinking of Pentecostals over the past thirty years, and I cannot believe it has all been for the good. When it becomes more important whether someone has spoken in tongues than whether he believes in the virgin birth, we have taken a step backward.

This is just one of the problems I believe Pentecostals must answer. I am not suggesting witch-hunting. I am suggesting that Pentecostals need to ask whether they are going to remain true to their evangelical roots. If they are, Scripture—not ecstatic experience—must define the limits to fellowship.

10

Can we learn from each other?

A re Pentecostals and non-charismatic evangelicals like east and west and "never the twain shall meet"? I wish I had a satisfactory answer to that question, but I do not. However, I do have some suggestions for both sides to think about, as I believe we can learn from each other.

My departure from the Pentecostal ministry was a traumatic event in my life. If I had been mistreated, it might have been easier. I made my exit with no bitterness. To cover my tracks, I asked for and received a letter from the district superintendent stating that I had left in good standing (see Appendix B).

Baptists and others can learn from Pentecostals. Unfortunately, many feel threatened by our Pentecostal friends. They accuse them of "sheep stealing," with some justification. Charismatics are missionaries who believe everyone needs their experience. Baptists, Nazarenes and just about anyone else are fair game. This open season policy has made others apprehensive of Pentecostals. In spite of this, a Baptist pastor or layperson will discover, more often than not, his Pentecostal counterpart is open to fellowship. He will most likely welcome being treated as a brother in Christ. In turn, as he recognizes your genuine commitment to Christ, he will likely look less upon your church as a hunting ground for converts.

Pentecostalism has changed radically from the storefront "holy roller" days. The most modern and attractive church edifices in a city are frequently Pentecostal. In fact, being a member of a particular Pentecostal church can even be a status symbol. The congregation may include lawyers, doctors and government leaders. Pentecostals are among the professors at leading interdenominational seminaries. The president of a major evangelical seminary near Boston is a member of the Assemblies of God.[1] There are very few evangelical congregations of any denomination without Pentecostal sympathizers. Pentecostal ministers are active in the leadership of many local clergy associations. We have come a long way from the time when the local clergy association in my hometown voted to exclude my father from membership.

Pentecostals are here to stay. As one of the fastest growing movements, the rest of us had better come to terms with their existence. Pentecostals have some strong points that are unrelated to their emphases on miracles and speaking in tongues. These strengths are, in my opinion, the key to their success.

One cannot help but be impressed with the commitment of Pentecostals. The reproach of being a Pentecostal has disappeared for the most part. Nevertheless, if someone is simply looking for a church to attend for the sake of appearance, they will probably not choose the Pentecostals. Too much involvement and commitment is expected. While Pentecostals have a rather high casualty rate for backsliders, the pews are not filled with nominal Christians. There is constant pressure to rededicate, reconsecrate, get refilled with the Spirit or to do something. It is difficult to remain a benchwarmer. This may be changing due to the size of some

---

[1] Robert E. Cooley (PhD) was president of Gordon-Conwell Theological Seminary from 1981 to 1997. Phil earned his MTS from Gordon-Conwell Theological Seminary in 1973.

Pentecostal churches, but I expect a survey would reveal a higher degree of involvement than most other churches.

The enthusiasm of Pentecostals cannot be ignored. Many churches have services that resemble pep rallies. While we want to avoid their excesses, our worship services need not resemble a wake. There is a wide range of music available today that is God-honouring and theologically correct, while contemporary in style. Suitable music can be found that appeals even to the young, without sacrificing biblical standards. Our Pentecostal friends are ahead of most of us in this field.

If there is one area I have noticed a difference between Pentecostals and other evangelicals more than anything else, it is in the area of prayer. Pentecostals know how to pray! I have always maintained that in most cases, the health of the average Pentecostal is not different from non-Pentecostals. However, if there are cases where Pentecostals do experience more healings, I believe it is due to prayer. I have found that many Baptists have no idea what is meant by "effectual fervent prayer" (James 5:16 KJV). Ask a Pentecostal about it and he or she will be quick to answer.

The noisiness of a Pentecostal prayer meeting is disturbing to some. When Pentecostals have a prayer meeting, everyone gets on their knees (we used to call them "prayer handles") and storms heaven. I have yet to become accustomed to prayer meetings where only a few pray because they cannot pray "nice prayers" or "pray in public." I always get some flak when I suggest this, but Pentecostals can teach the rest of evangelicals a lot about prayer.

There are side effects of prayer that sometimes outweigh the particular answer desired. I remember when a woman whom we all loved, contracted cancer while I was a Pentecostal pastor in St. Stephen, New Brunswick. She lived in Calais, Maine, but came to our church. Being a border town, we had a number of Americans in the church. When we heard the news, I called the church to pray. For weeks, we prayed almost continuously for her healing. We organized twenty-four-hour prayer chains, as well as special prayer times at church. She was a beautiful person and none of us wanted to lose her. I remember suggesting to the Lord that if he wanted to take someone, I had two or three other possibilities! She had no family in the area, except her husband who was a strange fellow and would not visit for fear of "catching the cancer." No one could reason with him, but people from the church were with her almost continually. We were sure God would heal her, but he did not.

During those last weeks in hospital, the night clerk called me on numerous occasions, as she would be asking for me. I would go to the hospital and find her in intense pain. Seated beside her, I would pray with her until she fell asleep, probably more from exhaustion than from the drugs. Usually, it would be 2 a.m. before I made my way down the dimly lit corridors and said goodnight to the desk clerk. I would walk out into the winter night, look up at the stars and ask, "Why?" One night, the call was not for me to come, but to inform me of her passing. I conducted her funeral and could offer no explanation except that One who loved her more than us wanted her to be with him.

That next year, we saw tremendous blessing on our church. I firmly believe we loved and prayed ourselves into a condition that God could bless. In the same way, I believe the blessing that many Pentecostal churches experience is not due to an emphasis on miracles, but an emphasis on prayer.

Another strong point of the Pentecostals is their openness to accept people of all classes and races. Pentecostal churches were some of the first to be integrated and most successful at making it work. Even before the civil rights movement, many Pentecostal churches were integrated. I did preach in some very bigoted white churches in the early sixties, but also in some that were successfully integrated. One of the nicest Thanksgiving meals I shared was at a African-American church in Chicago. I remember how the bishop and his wife made us feel so welcome. A number of white ministers were there and while one was obviously a bit uncomfortable, the rest of us enjoyed it. I wish I would have asked for the recipe for the cornbread dressing!

This family spirit is not the sole possession of Pentecostal churches. I have been blessed to pastor very warm and friendly Baptist churches, but I think the Pentecostals and the charismatic movement have helped break down reserve so we can more freely manifest affection for one another. I am not a hugger. I do not really feel comfortable with anything more than squeezing a hand or shoulder. It seems to me there has been an increased emphasis on loving one another and showing it in all evangelical churches in recent years. I think we have been influenced by the Pentecostals. While not given to affectionate displays beyond my immediate family, I can still relate to those who do. It is scriptural, as we see in John 13:35, "By this all people will know that you are my disciples, if you have love for one another" and in 1 Peter 5:14, "Greet one another with the kiss of love. Peace to all of you who are in Christ."

From the Pentecostal side, I believe they too have much to learn from non-charismatic evangelicals. I make these suggestions as a friend. They are the suggestions of an insider and family member. I say this because I find that I still resent attacks on Pentecostals, especially by those not intimately involved in the movement. My initial reaction is to think they do not know what they are talking about. I have never lost that family feeling. Family members may criticize one another, but do not let an outsider do it.

My first suggestion to Pentecostals would be to learn to live by *faith* and *fact* instead of by *feeling*. Sometimes we feel more married and more loving toward our spouse than at other times. However, we are not more married at some times than others. The fact of our legal commitment and relationship remains constant—all that changes is our feelings. Therefore, we should carry out our marriage and family responsibilities whether we feel like it or not. In the same way, sometimes we feel more Christian than at other times. Our relationship to Christ remains constant, based on his saving commitment to us. There are times when we need the joy of our salvation restored, but not the saving relationship (Psalm 51:12). The person who requires a continuously good feeling to serve the Lord is in trouble.

Feeling is important. That, nobody should deny, but feeling must be made subject to faith and not vice-versa. God is holy, just and good. Therefore, we must trust and follow him by faith, regardless of our feelings. We must do what is right, whether we feel like it or not.

The primary emphasis must be upon God and not us. The first question we must ask about a situation is not, "How do I feel about it?" but "How does *God* feel about it?" In turn, this demands an understanding of God's revealed Word, the Bible. To put it plainly but reverently, the source of discovering God's "feeling" is the Scriptures. While rejecting a merely intellectual religion, knowledge must take pre-eminence over feeling.

Baptists have been attacked for their doctrine of eternal security. Sometimes the attacks have merit. The idea that someone can make a profession of faith and then spend the rest of their life ignoring God, the church and the Bible while still on their way to heaven is insulting. The message of James, Jesus' half-brother and leader of the first church in Jerusalem, is clear: faith that does not change your life does not save your soul (James 2:14–20). James is in complete harmony with the apostle Paul in Titus 1:16, "They profess to know God, but they deny him by their works. They are detestable, disobedient, unfit for any good work."

At the same time, we recognize that heaven is attainable, not by *our* perseverance, but by *God's* perseverance (Philippians 1:6). Sinless perfection is not possible in this life. Therefore, salvation is only through grace. That in no way excuses sin in the life of a Christian; it must still be confessed and forsaken. Our goal is sinless perfection when we see Christ (1 John 3:2). We will never be satisfied with anything less. An old holiness minister was once asked, "Have you reached the place where you cannot sin?" "No," he replied, "but I have reached the place where I cannot enjoy it."

In the same vein, we need to restate that the Christian life should be a walk and not a pogo stick journey that jumps from experience to experience. The constant search for some new experience or excitement will eventually leave us dry. Having admitted the possibility of crises experiences, the spiritual life, like the physical, is one of gradual growth and development. We live in a day of "instants": instant coffee, instant breakfasts, instant soup, instant rice and so on. There is no such thing as instant spirituality or instant Christian maturity. No "second work of the Holy Spirit" will do it, only *discipleship* that learns and follows, in spite of the ups and downs in our feelings.

I would also suggest in this connection that Pentecostals need to become realists. While we can win battles with sin in this life, the war is never over. I once thought that someday I would reach the place of full victory over sin. I would be sort of out of danger, so to speak, but this never happens.

Frequently, it is suggested that the Christian should move out of the defeat of Romans 7 into the victory of Romans 8. At one time, I even taught this concept. I have now faced the reality that we live in Romans 7 our entire lives. Romans 7 and 8 are *both* the normal Christian life. The struggles of Romans 7 and the victory of Romans 8 *are* the testimony of a maturing Christian.

May I go so far as to suggest that Romans 7 presents a mature Christian rather than one who has not discovered the "secret" of victory? Paul writes Romans 7 in the present tense. I see three marks of maturity in Romans 7. First, he states the problem is with himself (7:15–18). He does not blame the law (7:12) or God or someone else. He places the blame squarely upon himself. That is a mark of a mature Christian. The immature Christian always blames someone or something else: the church, the pastor, the hypocrites or circumstances.

Second, he is aware of sin and hates it (7:15). Another mark of maturity is a consciousness and hatred of sin. The closer we are to God, the more aware of our sin we become. The immature Christian does not take sin seriously. The more we grow in Christ, the more hideous and unacceptable sin becomes. Romans 7 is the picture of a man who could not tolerate sin in his own life.

The third mark of the man in Romans 7 is that he recognizes he needs help beyond himself (7:24). There is no self-sufficiency in Romans 7. Paul knew his only source of help was Christ (7:25). He could then move to Romans 8 and talk about life in the Spirit, but it was not because he had eliminated the struggle with sin from his life. We must be realists. No "baptism" or "second work" can eliminate our struggle with sin. Our Lord wants us to lean on him for our entire lives. Does not the communion service remind us of the continuing need of the cross in our lives—"until he comes" (1 Corinthians 11:26)?

The subjectivity of Pentecostals also leaves them open to confuse their spirit with the Holy Spirit. They honestly believe it is the moving of the Holy Spirit, when it is actually their own feelings. I was at a Thursday night prayer meeting at a Roman Catholic Church, Holy Ghost Parish, in East Providence, Rhode Island, in 1971. I remember being impressed with seeing over 400 people on that hot August evening in a building without air conditioning. I was also impressed with the testimony of some nuns who talked about finding peace, after failing to find it in church liturgy, penance and even the holy orders. It seems they had been reading their Bibles and discovered an amazing verse in the third chapter of John and verse sixteen. They spoke about simply trusting in Christ and finding the peace that, heretofore, eluded them. I am a Protestant of the old school and wondered why they did not immediately become a fundamental Baptist! However, their testimony struck a responsive chord with me.

The meeting was charismatic and included singing choruses, messages in tongues and some prophecies, as well as testimonies. I had noticed conveniently placed ashtrays throughout the room and, during the two-hour meeting, smoke could be seen curling up from some of the congregation. After a while, a man got up and gave a message in tongues and the interpretation. It was a command to "stop defiling their bodies" as they were doing "yes, this very night." I immediately said to myself, "He's a Pentecostal." I confirmed afterward that he was the Church of God-minister concerned about smoking.[2] I question whether it was his spirit or the Holy Spirit.

In the fellowship time afterward, I was discussing this with a man who was then a professor at Barrington College.[3] He is now a leading charismatic Episcopal clergyman in Darien, Connecticut. He laughed and told me about what happened a previous night. It seems a traditional Pentecostal had given a message in tongues. He was a bit slow on the draw and, before he could give the interpretation, a nun gave the interpretation. It was a message encouraging the worship of Mary. The Pentecostal was flabbergasted. I am not prepared to judge, but I think all of it was a product of their own spirits and not the Holy Spirit. What each wanted was what they got.

My next suggestion to Pentecostals, is that they can learn from non-charismatics how to really trust God. Pentecostals (and others), in their very worthy and sincere desire to do something great for God tend to force the issues. It is almost as if God needs help and does not really understand what is at stake. Who has not

---

[2] The Church of God referred to here should not be confused with other Church of God denominations. Phil was referring to the Holiness Pentecostal Church of God based out of Cleveland, Tennessee (https://churchofgod.org).

[3] The man referred to was Terry Fullam. This name was supplied by David Reed.

been turned off by the continual begging for money by some television preachers? It seems God tells them of a work that *must* be done, but then fails to finance it—that requires a telethon! If they can trust God for miracles, why not for a financial one that does not require begging? Pentecostals are not the only offenders who beg for funds, but they are leaders in this field.

We once had a man as a guest speaker at our church who had succeeded his father as teacher on a radio program headquartered in Grand Rapids, Michigan.[4] He later founded a television program, which was one of the top ten religious TV programs in the United States, seen on hundreds of stations. I have been impressed with its simple format of Bible teaching and no sensationalism. They have very high quality music and production values, but everything is low key. I was also impressed with the modest lifestyle of our guest. I had been waiting for the opportunity, so I asked him, "Why do you never ask for money and seem to be succeeding while those who offer two or three miracles before breakfast, are always begging for money to survive?" He did not comment on the others I had referred to, but said this had always been their policy, initiated by his father.[5] When contributions to Radio Bible Class fall off, they cut back. When they increase, they expand. In other words, they trust God to determine the magnitude of their ministry. While it is a very high quality program, I believe the reason for its success in a competitive world is the blessing of God.

Is it possible Pentecostals might learn something about trusting God for miracles from those who are not charismatic? I think so. Look at the Saturday religion page in the newspaper in a large city and notice the church ads. Sometimes the religion section resembles the entertainment section. A typical example I have watched for some years is *The Toronto Star*. The ones at the forefront in offering some sensational attractions are the Pentecostal churches. Some must have a full time booking agent on the pastoral staff. Does the Holy Spirit need that much help? How did the church in the Book of Acts ever make it? What happened

---

[4] Phil was referring to Richard De Haan of Radio Bible Class fame and president of Our Daily Bread Ministries.
[5] Martin Ralph De Haan who founded Radio Bible Class.

to, "Not by might, nor by power, but by my Spirit" (Zechariah 4:6) that I used to hear so much about when I was younger?

I am only urging Pentecostals to ask some tough questions. Are those non-charismatic churches as "dead" as you think? Is what you have all that superior? After a campaign in Toronto with one of the major faith healers, and thousands reported healed, why can the religion editor of the *Toronto Star* offer a large cash reward for anyone proving they were healed—and get no takers?

My final word is this: These are not the questions of an enemy or a cynic. I still love my former brethren and miss them. These are the questions of one who was part of the Pentecostal movement for twenty-nine years. I discovered the questions; I have not been able to find the answers.

Epilogue

On Sunday, July 28, 2019, forty-five minutes before the first service began at Temple Baptist Church, Cambridge, Ontario, my father passed into the loving and resurrected arms of Jesus. It was appropriate he died on a Sunday because Dad loved church and wouldn't want to miss it, so he went straight from being with his family on earth to being with God's forever family worshipping up in heaven (Revelation 4–5). God had prolonged his days after a two year battle with cancer so that he could, in his own words, "Be a dying man preaching about the God-man who died on a cross for us." His last sermon was a month earlier when he preached on forgiveness.

Despite my having some amazing mentors along the way, I just wanted to be like my father. He was a loving man who served God, his family and church families faithfully with integrity and without much fanfare. He was my best friend, and for the last seven years of his life, I had one of the greatest gifts from God: to be able to serve alongside him as his fellow pastor. He was the teaching pastor and I was the lead pastor. He was my confidant and cheerleader, always deferring to me. Few retired pastors can let go and support their successor, but pastoring was never my father's identity. Christ was! Dad taught me to love and cling fast to God's Word. I think that was why I ended up preaching the two morning services and an evening service the Sunday my father died. I wanted to honour his commitment to God's Word and to lay down one's life for the sheep as he taught me, his father taught him and Jesus taught us all.

Fast forward to the summer of 2023, I was preparing to preach through 1 Corinthians. I wanted to help our church better understand the spiritual gifts. I remembered that back in the 1980s, my father wrote an unpublished book to record his journey from being a United Pentecostal pastor to a Fellowship Baptist pastor. I started reading it to my family on vacation, and we were all fascinated with his story. I thought others could be helped by the book, so I edited it along with my mother, Lelia, and sister, Stephanie. I told my friend and fellow elder Dr. Wayne Baxter about my father's book, and he encouraged me to see if I could get it published. Wayne loved my dad. I pitched the book to my colleague at Heritage College and Seminary, Dr. Michael Haykin. Michael was also enthusiastic about the book because it would teach those who are outside of the Baptist movement about the United Pentecostal Church in Canada. In the early twentieth century, some Baptists became Pentecostal. Phil's story is a Pentecostal "returning" to Baptist roots, while retaining an emphasis on prayer and being led by the Spirit.

Why publish this book now? Phil is in heaven and many of his contemporaries are already there with Jesus too. Those who were wrestling with whether to leave the United Pentecostal Church over the issues facing my father, would also have long-decided their pathway. Besides, Dad never wanted to take people with him on his theological journey. Though I think pastors and church leaders could be helped to learn some pastoral wisdom from this book, our family wanted to share the book with you for a few reasons. First, leaving a church or movement should not be done lightly. Leaving should be a very drawn out, heart-wrenching and prayerful decision that is based on whether God's Word or character is being violated. My father was patient and tried to bring about change, but knew he had changed and could no longer agree with his home church and denomination's views on issues such as the Trinity. Dad realized he could be Christ-centred, but not "Jesus only." He would say too many leave without first making "every effort to keep the unity of the Spirit through the bond of peace" (Ephesians 4:3 NIV). And when they do they leave "loudly" rather than quietly, as my father tried to do.

Secondly, the baptism of the Holy Spirit is often not understood in evangelical circles. It is often defined by what it is not (a work of God later on in the life of the believer) rather than what God is doing at the moment of salvation. Dad's treatment of the subject being baptized into Christ through the Spirit may be helpful. And thirdly, those trying to understand the spiritual gifts and their use today may also be helped by dad's book. Our big hope though is that when you are confused or confounded you keep your eyes on Jesus, the author and perfecter of our faith. He will always guide you down his path!

Jonathan Stairs

Lead pastor, Temple Baptist Church, Cambridge, Ontario; adjunct professor at Heritage College & Seminary; National Council Chair of the Fellowship of Evangelical Baptist Churches of Canada

Acknowledgements

I want to first acknowledge my mother, Lelia, Phil's beloved wife of 53 years. She has provided insights and been a conscientious editor of the book. We also want to acknowledge Phil's daughter Stephanie, who was another editor to the book and a constant (okay, mostly constant) source of joy to Dad through the years. Thanks for your keen eye and great memory, Steph. Tim Roddick (Steph's husband) was another editor whose eagle eye caught typos others missed. Thanks, Tim, for your endorsement as a pastor and church planter. Dad would be proud of you and your children, Danica and Brodie.

I also want to acknowledge my wife, Lori Stairs, whose sharp theological mind and articulate writing aided this project. Phil "aka Papa" would want us to acknowledge our daughter Jessie and her husband Andrew McElrea and their children Peyton and Ivy. Our sons, Josiah, Noah and Luke, also encouraged this project and we leave this memoir as a spiritual legacy for them to follow

Christ. Their eager interest in the book was a gentle nudge to sharing Dad's book with others.

I would be remiss to not thank Dr. Wayne Baxter who loved my father and thought we should pursue getting his book published. Wayne's recommendation of Dr. Michael Haykin was a massive step toward the completion of this book. Without Michael's support and cheerleading of this publication, we would still be contemplating self-publishing. Thanks, Michael, for taking a risk with this book and suggesting we add pictures. And then there is Janice Van Eck who has done a masterful job of taking a rough manuscript and making it look professional.

Our gratitude also goes to Dr. David Reed whose friendship with Dad goes back to their teenage days. David's Foreword in the book and helpful explanation of the UPC's understanding of the Trinity was extremely helpful and led me on a greater dive into understanding the Trinity.

Dad's endorsers, friends and colleagues Rev. Doug Blair, Rev. Dr. David Barker, Rev. Dr. Rick Cryder, Rev. Dr. Rick Baker, Rev. Dr. Norm Millar and Rev. Steve Jones evidence the impact Dad had on them and the significance of his story.

Brenda Laird also deserves recognition for being the typist of the original manuscript in the 1980s. Thank you so much for your service to Emmanuel Baptist Church, Chatham, and to Dad as his administrative assistant.

Dad served many churches through the years, and we want to acknowledge their support of his ministry, as they embraced his dry wit and spiritually rich preaching.

Most of all, I want to acknowledge God the Father, his Son Jesus and the Holy Spirit, for saving Dad and all of us who trust in Christ alone for salvation. It is because of Jesus that we will see Phil again, and there will be no more separation over doctrine and our only confession will be Christ as Lord!

A grateful son,
Jonathan Edward Stairs
July 30, 2025

Appendix A

WORDS OF PRAISE TO RECEIVE THE HOLY GHOST

Jesus who baptized 120 believers with the Holy Ghost on the day of Pentecost 10 days after He ascended to Heaven, is still baptizing Christians with the Holy Ghost today. Acts 2: 1-4.

Usually Jesus baptizes believers with the Holy Ghost while they are praising the Lord, and their words change from words of Praise to unknown tongues, which is proof that they have received the Holy Ghost.

We suggest these words of Praise to use while seeking the Baptism. To try to say words of Praise too perfectly hinders the Holy Ghost from speaking in His Heavenly languages thru you. SAY THE WORDS OUT LOUD'

As you praise God, do NOT try to stop stammering. In fact the more you get the words of praise mixed up, the easier it is for the Holy Ghost to take control of your tongue and speak in unknown tongues thru you. Isaiah 28: 11: "For with stammering lips and another tongue will I speak to this people."

TO START SEEKING

Say the words of Praise in a paragraph below over and over very rapidly for 2 or 3 minutes, then go to the next paragraph, repeating the words of Praise in each paragraph about the same length of time.

After you have repeated the words in all of the paragraphs, you may start at the beginning, and use these words of praise over and over.

1. GLORY TO GOD, HALLELUJAH   GLORY TO GOD HALLELUJAH   GLORY TO GOD

2. PRAISE PRECIOUS JESUS, PRINCE OF PEACE,   PRAISE PRECIOUS JESUS

3. I LOVE YOU JESUS   I LOVE YOU JESUS   I LOVE YOU JESUS, I LOVE YOU

4. JESUS SAVIOUR SAVE SINFUL SOULS, SANCTIFY SAINTS TO SERVE THEE

5. PRAISE GOD THE FATHER, GOD THE SON AND GOD THE HOLY GHOST.   PRAISE

6. I BESEECH BLESSED BAPTIZER BESTOW BOUNTIFUL BAPTISMAL BLESSINGS

7. GLORY TO JESUS   GLORY TO JESUS   GLORY TO JESUS   GLORY TO JESUS

8. WHILE WHOLEHEARTEDLY WORSHIPPING, WILLINGLY WAITING, JESUS BAPTIZE ME WITH THE HOLY GHOST.   WHILE WHOLEHEARTEDLY WORSHIPPING

9. GLORY TO GOD, GRACIOUS GENEROUS GIVER OF GOOD GIFTS.   GLORY TO GOD

PRAISE WORDS IN OTHER LANGUAGES TO REPEAT AS ABOVE

SPANISH	GERMAN	LATIN
GLORIA A DIOS ALLELUJAH Glory to God, Hallelujah	EHRE DEM GOTT, HALLELUJA	GLORIAM DEO HALLELUIA
ALABANZA AL SEÑOR Praise the Lord	DANKET DEM HERRN HALLELUJA	HALLELUIA CELEBRATE JEHOVAH
GLORIA A JESÚS Glory to Jesus	EHRE DEM JESUS	GLORIAM JESUM
YO TE AMO JESÚS I love you Jesus	ICH LIEBE IRH JESUS	EGO QUOD JESUM
BENDIGO A DIOS ALLELUJAH Bless God Hallelujah	GELOBT DER HERR HALLELUJA	BENEDIC JEHOVAE HALLELUIA

Repeat Praise Words out loud. If you begin to get tired, lay this sheet aside and use it later, or the next day, but don't give up.

PRAISE REPORT TO SEEK THE BAPTISM WITH THE HOLY GHOST

WRITE THE NUMBER OF MINUTES YOU PRAISE THE LORD EACH DAY, AND WRITE THE TOTAL NUMBER OF MINUTES ON THE BOTTOM LINE, WHEN FINISHED.

SUN.	MINUTES	PRAISED	SUN.	MINUTES	PRAISED
MON.	MINUTES	PRAISED	MON.	MINUTES	PRAISED
TUES.	MINUTES	PRAISED	TUES.	MINUTES	PRAISED
WED.	MINUTES	PRAISED	WED.	MINUTES	PRAISED
THURS.	MINUTES	PRAISED	THURS.	MINUTES	PRAISED
FRI.	MINUTES	PRAISED	FRI.	MINUTES	PRAISED

TOTAL NUMBER OF MINUTES OF PRAISE

The Baptism of the Holy Ghost is usually received while praising God. If you start to stammer and get words of Praise mixed up and other words and sound come in between words of Praise, don't stop, pause or hesitate, but continue until the Holy Ghost is speaking a clear language in unknown tongues, and then you may know that Jesus has baptized you with the Holy Ghost.

Be sure to write the date that you receive the Holy Ghost and also write any comments about it, because we are interested, and would like to rejoice with you when we know that Jesus has baptized you with the Holy Ghost.

Acts 11: "..on the Gentiles also was poured out the gift of the Holy Ghost, For they heard them speak with tongues, and magnify God." WRITE DATE HERE _____ when you received the Holy Ghost, and mail this sheet to us, also your Testimony.

Appendix B

United Pentecostal Church [Inc.]
MARYSVILLE, N. B.

BOARD:
A. W. POST
R. G. PRIEST
P. A. MacDONALD
C. B. DUDLEY
R. D. FOSTER
J. D. MEAN

SUPERINTENDENT:
E. P. WICKENS

SECRETARY-TREASURER
R. A. BEESLEY

REPLY TO:
928 Smythe Street
Fredericton, N.B.
Canada.

Nov. 1, 1971.

TO WHOM IT MAY CONCERN.

        This is to state that Rev. Philip Stairs has been with the United Pentecostal Church Inc. (Maritime) for a number of years, pastoring successfuly two churches, Implimenting a building program and errecting a new edifice in his last charge.

        He leaves us in good standing and held in high regard, Sincerely praying God may bless in what ever field he may feel lead to labour in.

Sincerely Yours

[signature]
Superintendent

Appendix C

U. P. C. Home Mission News

Authorized as 2nd Class Mail by th e Post Office Department, Ottawa, and for payment of postage in cash

Vol. XVI No. 6   BACK BAY, N. B.   FEBRUARY, 1968

Rev. Philip Stairs, B. A.

"Why I Am Still Pentecostal"

(PASTOR, ST. STEPHEN PENTECOSTAL CHURCH, ESPECIALLY WRITTEN FOR NEWSLETTER)

"Are you still Pentecostal?" was a question I was often asked after returning home from five years in the United States. This question was understandable in view of the fact that, after being reared in a Pentecostal minister's home, I had gone away to a inter-denominational Bible school and then a college, neither of which were favourable toward our Pentecostal teaching. Therefore, this question awaited me upon my return home. I had started with the idea of just obtaining a college education but had later decided to enter the ministry.

I decided to sit down and write just why I am "still Pentecostal." First of all, I would like to point out things that are not the reason for my still being Pentecostal. It is not because I consider Pentecostal people or churches perfect. I am fully aware of our short-comings. This treasure is in "earthern vessels", not vessels of steel or vessels of gold. Therefore, although this Pentecostal treasure is perfect, the vessel is neither perfect or break-proof.

Neither am I still Pentecostal simply for the sake of my parents. Although I have come to realize that my father knows considerably more than I thought he did a few years ago, if I were convinced that this way was not the right way, I would not hesitate to go elsewhere. Nor, is it because I think that no one besides Pentecostals have had any experience with God. God has not resigned and appointed me judge. I have met many who are sincerely seeking the Lord and I am not in a position to judge either their experience or their standing. God is fully capable of doing that.

Turning now to the positive side, the first reason I am still Pentecostal is the most important one. It is because of the teaching of the Bible, God's infallible Word. Truth must be judged, not by experience, but first of all by the scriptures. Using the Bible, whether in Greek, Hebrew, or English, no one has been able to convince me that this Pentecostal experience is not scriptural. In the book of Acts, there are five major occasions where people were filled with the Holy Spirit. In three of them (Acts 2:4; 10:46; 19:6), it definitely states that they spoke in tongues. In the fourth, which concerns Paul (Acts 9:17), it doesn't state there that he spoke in tongues, but Paul later testified to the fact that he spoke in tongues "more than ye all." (1 Cor. 14:18) In the fifth instance (Acts 8:17), it doesn't say that they spoke in tongues, but something unusual happened so that Simon immediately wanted to buy the power of giving the Holy Spirit. Certainly Simon would not have been interested in buying it if all Peter and John had done was laid hands on the people and said, "Now, by faith you have received the Holy Spirit." In light of these incidents in the book of Acts, the Pentecostal experience is certainly scriptural and I have been shown nothing in the Bible to convince me that this was "only for the Apostles' day."

The second reason I am still Pentecostal is because of my personal experience. At the age of nine, God filled me with His Spirit at a Saturday night men's prayer meeting. I spoke in tongues then and a few days later in another prayer meeting I spoke in tongues again. On this occasion there was an old coloured missionary there whom we called mother Holmes. After I was finished praying she told me that she had laboured for many years in a certain tribe that had a very difficult language, one that she had never mastered, and that night I spoke it as fluently as a native. She told me that I preached a sermon from 1 John on "God is Love". Now this would have to be either of God or of the Devil and no one could convince me that God would allow the Devil to possess a nine year old boy who was sincerely seeking to be filled with more of God. This experience stood by me in later years so that no one could convince me that speaking in tongues was just "gibberish."

The third reason that I am still Pentecostal is one that would not cut much ice with most people. It is just this: I simply like Pentecostal people and Pentecostal church-

(Continued on page 6)

135

FUNERAL SERVICE

On December 6, 1967, Bro. Eben A. Graham of Kirkland, N. B. was called home to be with the Lord. He was born in Harten Settlement on April 8, 1905, son of late Alex and Lottie (MacArthur) Graham and was a devoted supporter of United Pentecostal Church at Maxwell.

Funeral services were held from his late home, Pastor Hadley Rogers conducted the service. Burial was at MacKenzie Corner, N. B. He is survived by a brother, William Graham, Debec, and four sisters, Alma, Mrs. Elmer MacPherson, Chipman, Alice, Mrs. Hazen Kerr, Debec, Katie, Mrs. Fred Gray, Hartland and Helen, Mrs. Wesley James, Port Credit, Ontario. Bro. Graham will long live in the minds of those who knew him and his testimony will be cherished.

WHY I AM STILL PENTECOSTAL

(Continued from page 1)

es the best. In spite of all our faults and differences, I believe that we Pentecostal people have the best fellowship in the world. I like our Pentecostal preachers and think that they are the finest bunch of preachers you can find! I like our Pentecostal churches where we sing songs that have life to them and are not bound to a rigid pattern of worship found in some prayer book. I like our Pentecostal prayer meetings where we all pray together instead of praying individually, which usually ends up in each person trying to say a nicer prayer than the next one, and the ones who can't pray "nice prayers" don't take part.

So I am still Pentecostal and I expect to remain Pentecostal as long as Pentecost remains what it started out to be.

Bibliography

Bach, Marcus. *The Inner Ecstasy: The Power and Glory of Speaking in Tongues*. New York: World Publishing, 1969.

Bruce, F.F. *The Epistle to the Hebrews*. Grand Rapids: Eerdmans, 1964.

Duin, Julia. "The Holy Spirit and World Evangelization." *Christianity Today* (September 4, 1987): 45

Gaines, Steven S. *Marjoe*. New York: Dell Publishing Company, 1973.

MacDonnell, Wendy. "Jeffrey," *Young Ambassadors* (October 1985): 50ff.

Murray, Iain H., ed. *Sermons of the Great Ejection*. London: Banner of Truth, 1962.

Reynolds, Ralph and Joyce Morehouse. *From the Rising of the Sun. A History of the Apostolic Truth Across Canada and the Reflections of a Pioneer Preacher*. Surrey: Conexions, 1998.

Samarin, William J. "Glossolalia." *Psychology Today* (August 1982): 48ff.

Sherrill, John L. They Speak With Other Tongues. New York: Pyramid Publications, 1964.

Discover other titles from Heritage Seminary Press

The Way and the Water: Exploring Baptistic Roots
By Henk Bakker

In *The Way and the Water*, Dr. Bakker examines the history of the Baptist and Anabaptist movements, intertwined as they were in their formation, and as they arose out of persecution and the fight for religious freedom in Europe and beyond. In their struggle against state-enforced orthodoxy, they challenged the superstitions of medieval Christianity and sought to showcase the true nature of salvation and its outworking in the lives of believers, first in believer's baptism, and then in radically reoriented lives—with the way of Christ at its centre. For this, many of them suffered greatly.

It is hoped this title will encourage Baptist and Anabaptist communities to learn more about their history and consider how they can learn from each other's traditions. May it challenge us to live for Christ with greater commitment, engagement and endurance in society today.

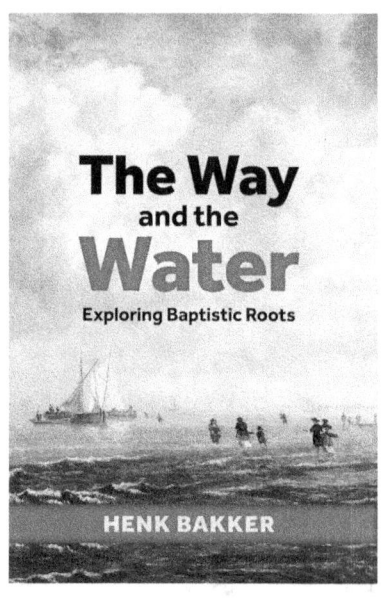

Translated by Aize Smit

ISBN 978-1-77484-171-6 (Pbk)
ISBN 978-1-77484-172-3 (eBook)
312 pages; 5.5 x 8.5"
Published September 2025

An imprint of H&E Publishing
heritageseminarypress.com

Discover other titles from Heritage Seminary Press

A Theologian in Service of the Church: The Collected Writings of Stanley K. Fowler
Edited by Michael A.G. Haykin & Jonathan N. Cleland
Volume 1 & Volume 2

For over fifty years, the writings of Stanley K. Fowler, long-time professor of theological studies at Central Baptist Seminary, Toronto, Ont., and then Heritage College & Seminary, Cambridge, Ont., have informed and clarified theological issues for Baptists in Ontario, Canada and beyond.

Using careful biblical exegesis to address issues facing the church—such as baptism, local church autonomy, public ethics, divine sovereignty and human freedom and divorce and remarriage—Dr. Fowler has sought to equip Christians to serve the Lord well.

In this two-volume collection of his works, the editors hope the church can continue to learn from his insightful handling of the Word of God and enter deeper into relationship with the Word made flesh, Jesus Christ.

Volume 1
ISBN 978-1-77484-160-0 (Hdcvr)
ISBN 978-1-77484-157-0 (Pbk)
ISBN 978-1-77484-158-7 (Ebook)
276 pages; 5.5 x 8.5"
Published January 2025

Volume 2
ISBN 978-1-77484-163-1 (Hdcvr)
ISBN 978-1-77484-161-7 (Pbk)
ISBN 978-1-77484-162-4 (Ebook)
296 pages; 5.5 x 8.5"
Published May 2025

An imprint of H&E Publishing
heritageseminarypress.com

Discover other titles from Heritage Seminary Press

A "phoenix of women" Puritan spirituality in the letters of Brilliana Harley
Introduced and edited by Michael A.G. Azad Haykin

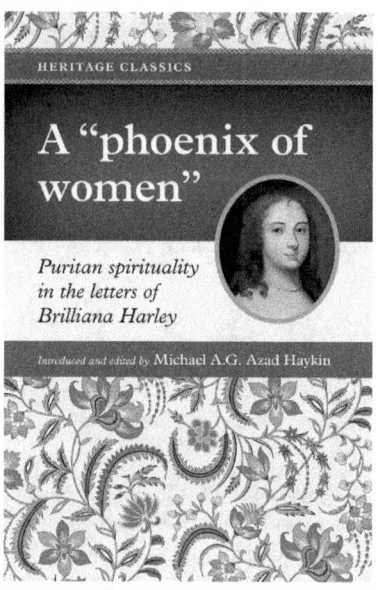

The life of Lady Brilliana Harley was marked by a deep and living relationship with God. A Puritan Presbyterian by conviction, Brilliana was shunned by her neighbours during the tumultuous English Civil Wars and is remembered as valiantly resisting the siege of her home by the forces of Charles I.

Brilliana's letters reveal the heart of her spirituality. While concerned about her son Edward (Ned)'s studies at Oxford, his diet and exercise, she especially encourages him about the value of a vital relationship with God. Her letters also expose the breadth of her reading and her theological acumen. As the troubles around her increased, she took increasing solace in the truths of election, the sufficiency of Christ's work and the sovereignty of God. The soil of her heart was truly warmed by "the sweet waters of God's Word."

ISBN 978-1-77484-152-5 (Pbk)
ISBN 978-1-77484-153-2 (Ebook)
172 pages; 5.5 x 8.5"
Heritage Classics
Published September 2024

An imprint of H&E Publishing
heritageseminarypress.com

Discover other titles from Heritage Seminary Press

The oversight of souls: Essays on pastoral ministry
By Ray Van Neste

How do you understand pastoral ministry? What is the centre of your calling as a pastor? Is it difficult for your people to speak directly with you? Do you know your sheep? Do they know you?

In this book, Ray Van Neste looks to God's Word and church history to show that the oversight of souls is to be the very *heart* of pastoral ministry. The author of Hebrews writes that congregants are to: "Obey your leaders and submit to them, for they are keeping watch over your souls, as those who will have to give an account" (Hebrews 13:17). This guarding, shepherding and watching over souls requires knowledge of and meaningful engagement with the sheep and seeing them as "very dear to us" (1 Thessalonians 2:8), with the goal to "present everyone mature in Christ" (Colossians 1:28).

ISBN 978-1-77484-154-9 (Pbk)
ISBN 978-1-77484-155-6 (Ebook)
130 pages; 5.5 x 8.5"
Published October 2024

An imprint of H&E Publishing
heritageseminarypress.com

Discover other titles from Heritage Seminary Press

Losing Your Luggage: Finding Freedom from Sinful Baggage
By Rick Reed

Losing Your Luggage takes you on a journey through Romans 6–8, helping you find freedom from the sinful baggage that weighs you down. Your guide for this trip is Rick Reed, who brings out practical, down-to-earth wisdom from Paul's letter as he walks alongside you on this journey. He is one who speaks from experience and is a helpful guide to show you the main sights and lessons of these important chapters. Journey toward greater joy and freedom in Christ—and lose some sinful baggage along the route!

ISBN 978-1-77484-120-4 (Pbk)
ISBN 978-1-77484-121-1 (Ebook)
104 pages; 6 x 9"
Published June 2023

An imprint of H&E Publishing
heritageseminarypress.com

Discover other titles from Heritage Seminary Press

Life is Worship: A *festschrift* in honour of Douglas A. Thomson
Editors: David G. Barker & Michael A.G. Haykin

These essays honour the life and ministry of Dr. Doug Thomson who, as a teacher, pastor, colleague and music leader, has influenced countless lives and congregations in Ontario, Canada, and beyond. The subjects of these chapters cover themes that are precious in the life of the church—revealing how all of life is worship.

Topics include expositions of psalms and hymns, the theology of worship, spirituals, hallmarks of a worship leader, friendship in the composition of hymns, lament, etc.—even some sermons for Easter weekend. It is hoped that these essays will encourage discussion, promote the development of an understanding of the theology around worship, challenge readers to think deeply about this crucial area and, most of all, bring glory and praise to our great God.

ISBN 978-1-77484-128-0 (Pbk)
ISBN 978-1-77484-129-7 (Ebook)
364 pages; 6 x 9"
Published September 2023

An imprint of H&E Publishing
heritageseminarypress.com

Discover other titles from Heritage Seminary Press

Paul and His Christian Mission
By Michael Azad A.G. Haykin
Includes Study Guide

The mission of the apostle Paul is central to the New Testament, where it was vital in the establishment of the early church and spreading the gospel throughout the world of his day. This study provides a concise but rich view of Paul the man and Paul the missionary. At his conversion to Christ, Paul was given a clear mandate to bring the gospel to the Gentiles. Paul loved the church, and he was zealous to win the lost to Christ. He appreciated and cultivated co-labourers in the work of the gospel, as he depended on the power of the Holy Spirit.

Paul's experience challenges the reader. Study guide questions are provided to help reflect on and apply the things that are learned in this short, focused study of Paul's life.

ISBN 978-1-77484-106-8 (Pbk)
ISBN 978-1-77484-107-5 (Ebook)
88 pages; 5.5 x 8.5"
Published December 2022

An imprint of H&E Publishing
heritageseminarypress.com

Discover other titles from Heritage Seminary Press

This Poor Man Called: Stories and Songs of David
Volume 1 & Volume 2
By David G. Barker

David Barker takes a unique approach in this exploration of the psalms of David. Each chapter begins with a creative retelling of the biblical narrative, setting the scene for the psalm arising out of that experience. Having grounded the psalm in the "story," Barker then goes into a verse-by-verse exposition of the psalm, and provides some explanatory notes and a statement of the key message of the psalm.

At the end of each psalm exposition, Barker asks three basic questions: What do we learn about God? What do we learn about ourselves as the people of God? and What do we learn about the world? Answering these questions helps us to understand how David's experience shaped his theocentric and biblical worldview.

Volume 1
ISBN 978-1-77484-063-4 (Pbk)
ISBN 978-1-77484-064-1 (Ebook)
122 pages; 5.5 x 8.5"
Published Spring 2022

Volume 2
ISBN 978-1-77484-110-5 (Pbk)
ISBN 978-1-77484-111-2 (Ebook)
192 pages; 5.5 x 8.5"
Published February 2023

An imprint of H&E Publishing
heritageseminarypress.com

Dominus Deus fortitudo mea | The sovereign LORD is my strength